The American Playhouse in the Eighteenth Century

The Park Theater, New York. Watercolor by John C. Hind, 1809. Courtesy of the Harvard Theatre Collection.

The American Playhouse in the Eighteenth Century

by Brooks McNamara

Harvard University Press

Cambridge, Massachusetts

1969

For Monroe Lippman

Preface

From the construction of the first American playhouse at Williamsburg, Virginia, about 1716, to the end of the eighteenth century, more than seventy theaters were used by amateur and professional players. Studies of several of the best known buildings have appeared from time to time, and information about more obscure buildings may be found in local histories, books on theatrical activity in various towns and cities, and, of course, in the diaries, letters, and newspapers of the period. But no book has drawn together the most important of these accounts in order to study the evolution of the early American playhouse.

In tracing the development of the theater building in the colonies and the new nation, I have made no attempt to create exhaustive annals of the American playhouse, but have concentrated on delineating and interpreting the major patterns of expansion and change that characterized the work of the theater-builder in the eighteenth century. The task has not been an easy one. No eighteenth-century structure intended primarily as a theater exists today. Many of the records concerned with the design, construction, and decoration of the earliest playhouses have been lost or destroyed, and the contemporary accounts that have survived are often fragmentary and vague. It has sometimes been quite impossible to describe the appearance of an early theater or to evaluate its importance to the growth of theater-building in this country. For this reason I have not commented on every playhouse erected in America in the eighteenth century. Nor have I felt it necessary to discuss the many taverns, courthouses, and inns that were temporarily converted to playhouses unless it could be shown that substantial changes were made to accommodate theatrical production. The discovery of a number of new sources, however, has made it possible to correct errors and misconceptions found in earlier accounts, and to shed new light on some neglected examples of early theater architecture in America.

For criticism of this study I am obligated to Professor Paul Hostetler of the Department of Speech and Dramatic Arts, Temple University, and Professor George Hendrickson of the Department of Theater at Tulane University. For suggestions and help I am particularly grateful to Professor Hugh Rankin of the Department of History at Tulane, whose able research in the field of colonial American theater history provided the point of departure for this volume. I am grateful also to Colonial Williamsburg, Tulane University, and the University of Delaware, whose research grants helped to make this study possible, and to the many librarians and archivists who aided me in my work.

For advice and encouragement I am grateful to Paul Buchanan, John Selby, E. M. Riley, and Milo Naeve of Colonial Williamsburg; Richard Doud of the Henry Francis du Pont Winterthur Museum; Robert Land of the Library of Congress; Miss Helen Willard of the Theatre Collection, Harvard University; and the late George Freedley. Yale University, the Folger Shakespeare Library, the Library of the American Institute of Architects, the Walter Hampden Memorial Library of the Players' Club, and the Henry Francis du Pont Winterthur Museum generously provided additional research materials. Special thanks go to my wife for her kindness and patience, to Betsy Meade for her unfailing good humor during the typing of drafts of this book, and to Babotto Montgomery for reading proof

A short version of the Introduction to this book appeared originally in *The Connoisseur,* December 1967, as "The English Playhouse in Eighteenth-Century America." Much of the material in Chapters III and IV was first published as "David Douglass and the Beginnings of American Theater Architecture," in *Portfolio III,* 1967, the annual publication of the Winterthur Museum. The material used in the *Connoisseur* and *Portfolio* articles is reprinted here with the kind permission of the publishers.

My debt to numerous authors of books, monographs, and articles I have tried to acknowledge in the notes. These acknowledgments would be incomplete, however, without a word on the work of two English theater historians, Miss Sybil Rosenfeld and Richard Southern. Miss Rosenfeld's writings on the English provincial stage and on the fair booth theaters have provided me with many valuable insights into the probable nature of America's earliest theater buildings. I have, in one case, disagreed with Mr. Southern's conclusions regarding the nature of an American playhouse; yet my debt of gratitude to him is incalculable, for without his splendid books and articles on English theater architecture and stage machinery my own work would have been virtually impossible.

New York University   Brooks McNamara
September 1968

Contents

Illustrations

xv

xvii

The American Playhouse in
the Eighteenth Century

Introduction

Throughout the whole of the eighteenth century there was no significant influence on the American theater building that did not have its origin somewhere in the English traditions of stage-craft and theater architecture. It is likely, however, that early amateur theaters like the playhouse constructed at Williamsburg about 1716 and Charleston's Dock Street Theater of 1736 were related to English theater architecture in only the most general way. If these first amateur buildings resembled English theaters at all, it is probable that they were most similar to the simple booths used for theatrical productions at English fairs.

The reasons for the temporary nature of these earliest buildings are clear enough: there was neither the time, the money, the technical knowledge, nor the cultural impetus to construct first-rate permanent playhouses. Theatrical activity before the arrival of the first English company at mid-century was totally amateur, and it would have been the purest folly to erect expensive buildings for an activity so incidental to the day-by-day life of colonial towns and villages.

Although a troupe of so-called professional players under the leadership of Walter Murray and Thomas Kean was organized in 1749, it was only with the appearance in 1752 of a small English acting company led by Lewis Hallam that truly professional theater entered the colonies. Professional theater architecture did not follow immediately in the wake of the English players, however. The first homes of these early actors were temporary quarters little better than the amateur playhouses constructed in the first half of the eighteenth century. Until some amount of working capital and some degree of community interest had been obtained there was little point in erecting a substantial theater, even if the money for its construction could have been found by the manager.

In some cases, of course, the first players followed the simplest possible expedient, merely renting a convenient room or an empty building and constructing within it a simple stage for their performances. A pair or two of side wings and a back cloth, together with a piece of green baize for a front curtain and a few loose benches for audience seating, were all that was absolutely necessary to a theatrical performance. Quite probably productions of which we have no record took place in barns and inns around the countryside without even these simple items of theater furniture.

With the Hallam company, however, the basic form of the eighteenth-century English playhouse was established in the colonies. Indeed, the development of the colonial playhouse from the arrival of the Hallams to the Revolution illustrates no fundamental changes in the design of the theater building. Apparent instead is a slow and somewhat painful progress reflecting the cultural progress of the colonies themselves. It is possible, of course, to overstate the essential barrenness of life in the thirteen English colonies after mid-century; yet it is plain that forces present in colonial culture retarded the growth of theater building throughout the third quarter of the eighteenth century. Although the period of actual pioneer existence was rapidly disappearing in many parts of the colonies, the financial security and leisure necessary to the promotion of any branch of the arts was only beginning to develop. Towns remained small and a theater established in any town was faced with serious operating difficulties. Though such a theater could depend upon some patronage for each of its physical—and sociological—divisions of boxes, pit, and gallery, the long working hours and the poverty and ignorance of many sections of the population resulted in a total lack of interest from some quarters. Neither Hallam's company nor the later colonial troupe organized by David Douglass, who married Hallam's widow in 1758, could depend upon drawing a living from theatrical operations in a single colonial town. By necessity if not by choice the earliest companies were peripatetic, establishing playhouses where and when the opportunity arose. Such an unsettled existence scarcely lent itself either to consistency or permanence in building.

It is doubtful, in any case, that the money to erect a really fine theater building was available at all. Though it is true that there were individual colonists who possessed large fortunes for the time, there was no system of direct patronage that could have led to the construction of elegant private or semi-private playhouses like those found in many European principalities or in some towns in the British Isles. Aside from the managers themselves, there was no single individual sufficiently interested in either the cause or the financial rewards of theater to finance the construction of a public playhouse.

Of equal significance is the fact that the Hallam and Douglass companies possessed a virtual theater monopoly in the colonies. It was they who set the standard for theater buildings, and they were totally free from the spur of competition that might have led to more rapid progress in theater architecture. Douglass' best houses, Philadelphia's Southwark Theater of 1766 and the John Street Theater, erected in New York in 1767, were little better than the most ordinary English town theaters. Even if Hallam and Douglass had been challenged by other managers,

3

it is doubtful that their playhouses would have rivaled the best provincial houses of England; but the chances are good that they would have attempted to meet and surpass competition and that houses of higher quality would have appeared before the Revolution.

During and after the war there was neither the time nor the money to construct new playhouses; yet slowly English players began to return and by the middle eighties interest in theater building began to arise once again. An era of good theater architecture was about to begin. In large part the change for the better was bound up with changes in the character of American life. A new prosperity led ultimately to an awakening interest in the drama as a medium of cultural expression and as social recreation. At the same time the old Puritan view of plays and players was rapidly disappearing: though the actor and his art continued to be viewed with some suspicion in parts of New England, open hostility to the stage on religious and moral grounds was declining. The new nation had begun to accept and even promote the drama, and a native American theater was in the making. Although American actors and managers appeared in the later years of the eighteenth century, the stage continued to be largely dominated by representatives of the English theater; and the American playhouse remained, in all important respects, as thoroughly English as it had been in the period of Lewis Hallam and David Douglass. But the new English managers who arrived in America were better trained and possessed sounder financial backing than their predecessors. Managers like Thomas Wall, John Bignall, Thomas Wade West, and Thomas Wignell were the products of a prosperous provincial theater and they dreamt of playhouses that would have been inconceivable in the years before the war.

In small towns and villages, of course, undistinguished and even wretchedly inadequate theaters continued to be erected. But by 1800 playhouses like Boston's Federal Street Theater, Philadelphia's Chestnut Street Theater, and the Park Theater in New York equaled, in most respects, the finest English provincial houses. In the largest cities theater architecture was no longer so much the responsibility of the manager. Increasingly, trained architects assumed a larger part in playhouse design. The Federal Street Theater was the work of the distinguished American architect Charles Bulfinch, the Charleston Theater of 1793 was created by James Hoban, architect of the White House, and the Park Theater was probably designed by Joseph Mangin, who was responsible for the plans for the famous New York City Hall. In most important respects their designs conformed to late eighteenth-century English conventions of theater architecture, but they were no longer so clearly imitative. Had Benjamin Latrobe's 1798 designs for a theater at Richmond, Virginia, been translated into a finished playhouse, America would have possessed the finest and, in many respects, the most imaginative small playhouse in the English-speaking world.

I / The Amateur Period

One good Substantiall house commodious for Acting such
Plays as shall be thought fitt to be Acted there.
(William Levingston, 1716)

The years that followed the Commonwealth witnessed the development of a new and colorful English theater. Both plays and playhouses emerged as a striking rejection of the taste for plainness and solemnity that had characterized the Puritan Interregnum. But in the American colonies there was to be seen no hint of the elegance and vitality of the Restoration stage. An almost total theatrical vacuum existed throughout America in the final years of the seventeenth century. Not until the eighteenth century did the playhouse conceived in the reign of Charles II find its way to the New World; but when it did at last appear, the English playhouse dominated American theater architecture for the remainder of the colonial period.

The colonial playhouses of the earliest amateur period, however, were English only at second hand. These early theaters, in use before the arrival of the first professional acting companies, were probably little more than crude approximations of proper English playhouses, loosely based on travelers' accounts and a few stray illustrations of the London and provincial houses of the day, and on common-sense deductions about what a theater building ought to be. Only when the colonists had developed some leisure and, consequently, some degree of cultural sophistication did the inclination to support drama in any permanent way come to exist; only then did the first professional companies arrive, and with them the first truly professional theater buildings. Before the middle of the century no more than a handful of important towns possessed even the crudest playhouse. Both economic hardship and opposition to the stage made the construction of such essentially frivolous buildings virtually impossible outside the largest centers of population—and quite inconceivable in the New England colonies.

As early as the third quarter of the seventeenth century, however, the drama had begun to find a temporary home in the principal rooms of taverns and private dwelling houses. In 1665 a brief sketch or play, *Ye Bare and Ye Cubbe,* was produced on the eastern shore of Virginia, probably at Cowle's Tavern near Pungoteague; and in 1687 Judge Samuel Sewall of Boston wrote indignantly of an innkeeper who had fitted out a room with seats for a performance by a traveling conjurer.[1] The use of a hall or great room, of course, represented a simple solution to the problems of amateur theatrical production. In its most basic form such a temporary theater might be nothing more than the bare room fitted out with seats of which Sewall wrote. But for more elaborate productions a chamber in a prosperous inn or a large private house might for a few hours be transformed into a fairly respectable theater.

In 1739, for example, a temporary hall theater was created for a performance of a "New Pantomine Entertainment in Grotesque Characters" called *Harlequin and Scaramouch.* The pantomime, which was produced by Henry Holt, a dancing master, took place in the long room of the residence of Stephen De Lancey at the southeast corner of Broad and Pearl Streets in New York. At best, it is likely that the room was adapted to include a raised, curtained stage with a simple backdrop and wings somewhat similar to that shown in Hogarth's painting of a private performance of *The Indian Emperor* in 1731 (Fig. 1).[2]

Some pleasing effects could surely have been achieved by skilled amateurs in a temporary hall theater like that used by Holt, although one imagines that far worse rooms were more common. The chief difficulty of such an arrangement lay in the fact that the design of both stage and auditorium was rigidly controlled by the limitations of a room never intended as a theater. A permanent raised stage and proscenium arch of a desirable size, and a sloping auditorium floor, could scarcely be installed in a hall or great room. Thus, these earliest theaters were suitable only for a limited number of performances of the simplest sort. The answer to the problems presented by such temporary playhouses was, of course, the use of more or less permanent theaters in which a proper stage and adequate seating could be arranged.

It is likely that the two playhouses operated in the city of New York during the 1730's had little better facilities than the long room in De Lancey's house; yet both seem to have been intended as permanent or semi-permanent theaters. Probably both of them were housed in buildings converted from some commercial purpose. One of the playhouses, the "*New Theatre* in the building of the Hon. Rip Van Dam, Esq.," was in use in December of 1732.[3] Although its exact location is not clear, we know that Van Dam owned a structure of some sort located near the intersection of Pearl Street and Maiden Lane, and the early New York theater historian, T. Allston Brown, identifies the theater as a large room in the upper part of a building at the junction of these two streets.[4]

Only in 1735, however, was the location of a New York playhouse recorded with any certainty. A map of that date shows a

1 / A private performance of *The Indian Emperor*. Engraving by Robert Dodd after the painting of 1731 by William Hogarth, 1792.

structure labeled "Play House" on the east side of Broadway, just above Beaver Street (Fig. 2). That this was the New Theater mentioned three years earlier is unlikely, although definite evidence is lacking. Van Dam, a prosperous burgher of the city, owned property in various parts of New York, but his ownership of a building on this site has never been established. In any event, the 1735 map suggests that the structure at Broadway and Beaver Street was not originally intended as a theater. It is impossible to determine an exact scale for the Broadway building, but it is apparent that it was extraordinarily large—much larger, in fact, than Trinity Church, which stood on the opposite side of the street and two blocks farther up Broadway. It seems inconceivable that a theater for which there was no resident company would have been constructed on so grand a scale. The proximity of the "Play House" to the river would seem also to add to the possibility that it was originally erected as some sort of store or warehouse and that some portion of it was remodeled into a theater.

Probably both of these theaters were nothing more than rented space cheaply divided into a rough stage and auditorium. The chief virtue of such a plan lay in the fact that it was no longer necessary constantly to dismantle and reassemble the stage and its equipment; its chief defect was that some degree of improvisation within an existing room remained necessary. Yet, for amateur players presenting only an occasional performance, such an arrangement was probably adequate—and the only answer to the need for a permanent playhouse short of constructing a building expressly designed as a theater.

The construction of an actual playhouse was, in most cases, beyond the means of amateurs, who played only from time to time and could expect little if any financial reward for their efforts. Yet, in several instances, seemingly permanent buildings were erected to house productions by semi-professional

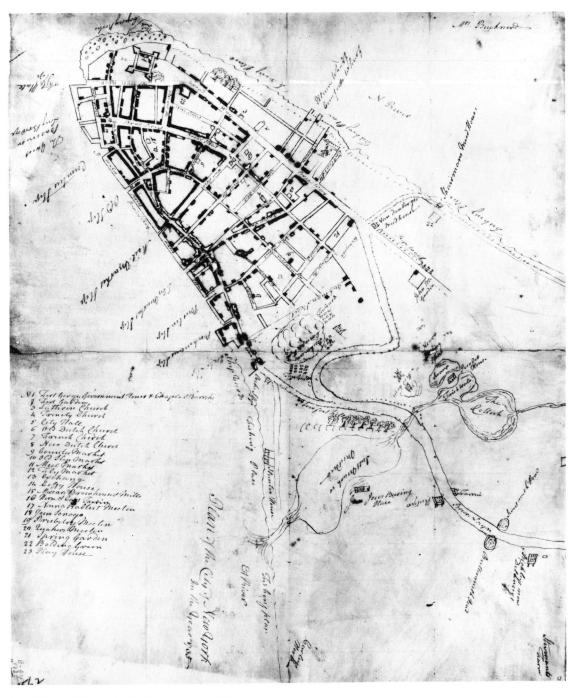

2 / Map of New York City in 1735. The playhouse is number 23.

performers. A curious little building, perhaps similar to the crudest sort of English fair booth, was erected in New York by 1749. This structure, which was probably designed for puppet plays rather than performances by live actors, was known only as a "large Theatrical Room, next to the sign of the Dolphin (built on Purpose) near the Work-House, in New York, for the entertainment of Gentlemen, Ladies, and Others." Apparently the Theatrical Room was arranged in the simplest possible manner, for the New York *Weekly Journal* advised the public that prices of admission to performances by Punch's Company of Comedians were: "Front Seats, two shillings. Middle seats, one Shilling and six Pence. Back Seats, one Shilling."[5]

An earlier theater, the New Booth on Society Hill, located just outside the Philadelphia city limits and in use by 1724, may have occupied a converted building of some sort.[6] But its name implies that the playhouse, which housed rope dancers and a Picklehering play, was much like the theater booths found at English fairs. These booths, although they sometimes approached the size and comfort of a relatively good playhouse, were frequently little more than crude frame buildings, unfinished and rather barren, in which traveling managers set up the paraphernalia of their trade. The English theater booth had developed out of the simple open-air stage with a curtained background behind. Early in the eighteenth century, however, both actors and audience were enclosed in the interior of the booth itself, although the earlier outdoor stage was retained and served as a kind of advertising platform on the front of the building. Hogarth's *Southwark Fair* (1733) shows such a booth theater, evidently constructed of wood and hung with colorful show cloths that advertised the booth's current offerings (Fig. 3).

The question of the interior appearance of such booth theaters is not so easily solved. It is probable, however, that an English watercolor dating from approximately 1780 illustrates the inte-

3 / Southwark Fair. Engraving by William Hogarth, 1733.

4 / A Puppet Show. Watercolor by W. H. Pyne, c. 1780.

rior of a fair booth playhouse. The painting (Fig. 4), shows a flat auditorium floor, with a low gallery that is apparently raked or stepped appearing behind what might be described as the pit area. The fact that the New Booth on Society Hill was similarly divided only into pit and gallery is perhaps further evidence that America's second playhouse was little more than the typical booth theater of the English fairs.[7]

The construction of theater buildings for purely amateur players was a rare event in the early eighteenth century, although several buildings appear to have been erected primarily for the use of local actors. Sometime between 1716 and 1718, America's first theater was constructed on the east side of the Palace Green at Williamsburg, Virginia, by William Levingston. Levingston, a merchant of New Kent and sometime dancing master, may have erected his playhouse with the idea of importing an English acting company to the colonial capital. In any case, Levingston asserted that he had "at his own Proper Costs & Charge Sent to England for Actors & Musicians for the better performance of the said Plays."[8] Yet there is no evidence that the actors whom Levingston claimed to have sent for ever appeared on American shores, and all of the recorded performances at the theater were by amateur players.[9]

It is possible that two of Levingston's servants, Charles and Mary Stagg, had been connected with the British stage before their indentures carried them to Virginia, for they were to operate their master's playhouse. But it seems unlikely that Levingston received much advice from trained men and women of the theater when time for construction of the playhouse arrived. Nor is it likely that he consulted any professional English designer concerning his idea for a theater, since Levingston was a man of modest means who could scarcely have afforded a designer's fee. There is the possibility, of course, that he had seen one of the great London theaters of the Restoration. It is even possible that some interested and influential Williamsburg amateur—

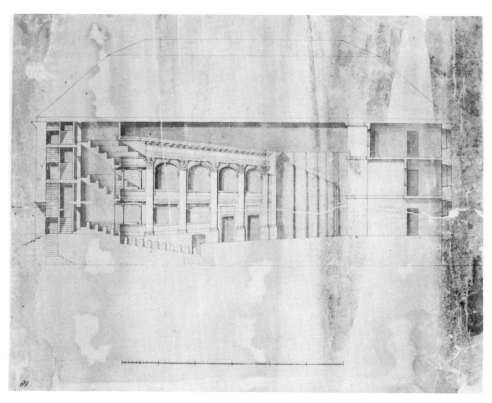

5 / Longitudinal section of a theater, probably the Theater Royal, Drury Lane. Ink and wash drawing by Christopher Wren, c. 1674.

perhaps Governor Spotswood himself—had sent for plans and drawings from England. The playhouse, for example, might have resembled a very simple version of London's famous Drury Lane, a theater erected in 1674, and probably based on a design by Christopher Wren (Fig. 5). There is as much reason to believe, however, that Levingston's playhouse did not resemble professionally designed theaters in anything but the most general way, and that no real prototype for the building existed in the British Isles.

Documents and archaeological evidence are of little help in unraveling the mystery of Levingston's playhouse. An archae-

16

ological survey of the theater site by Colonial Williamsburg indicates that the building stood on a brick foundation 30 feet 2 inches wide, and 86 feet 6 inches long, with the narrow side facing the Palace Green.[10] The foundations offer little information of significance except to suggest by their comparative lightness that they supported a wooden building rather than one constructed of brick. We do know, however, that the theater was converted to use as a Court of Hustings in 1745. An advertisement in the *Virginia Gazette* (Williamsburg) relating to proposed alterations of the building at that time indicates that it was indeed constructed of wood, weatherboarded, painted, and roofed with shingles. Evidently there were not sufficient doors or windows in the playhouse to allow its immediate conversion to a courtroom, for a door and "five large Sash windows" are called for in the advertisement.[11]

About the interior of the building the record is completely silent. No evidence of exterior doors or steps has been found to indicate the number or location of entrances to Levingston's theater, nor can much of value be determined from the placement of interior walls found in the excavation of the theater site (Fig. 6). It is quite impossible to tell whether Levingston's playhouse was a proper theater. If it did not resemble houses

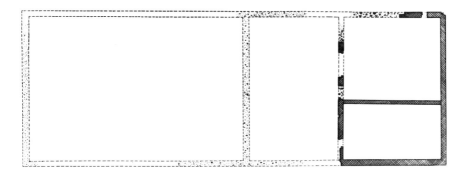

6 / Excavated foundations of Levingston's theater, Williamsburg, Virginia.

like Drury Lane in its overall plan, it was probably little better than a large booth theater or, at worst, a barn with some concessions made to the comfort of the audience and the convenience of the players. The evidence for such a supposition is not entirely lacking. Advertisements for performances at the theater do not mention prices for box, pit, and gallery seats, a significant though not conclusive indication that no such divisions existed.

If Levingston's playhouse did not contain a raked pit floor, then the typical arrangement of boxes, pit, and gallery could not have existed in the house, and some drastic modification of the conventional plan must have been employed. The evidence of several English buildings that were arranged in rather unorthodox ways suggests some possibilities for the appearance of Levingston's theater if it was only the crudest sort of amateur playhouse. A print, dated 1789, of a country theater (Fig. 7), shows a rough playhouse with an upper and lower gallery, both of which are presumably raked or stepped. A section at the left of the lower gallery area seems remarkably clear of spectators and suggests that entrance to the upper gallery was by a flight of steps placed there. A door visible in the left wall of the theater may well have been the sole entrance to this crude little rural playhouse.

The "pit" of the Country Theater is evidently no pit at all, but a flat floor with a miscellaneous collection of loose seats for the audience; and since the stage is not raised, a conventional placement of the orchestra just forward of the stage was impossible. For this reason the manager seems to have resorted to a device similar to the "Musique Room" found at Restoration playhouses like Dorset Garden, in which the orchestra was placed above the proscenium arch. Here, however, the musicians are suspended above the audience in a small gallery on the left wall of the auditorium.

The Country Theater is not unlike the supposed fair booth interior mentioned earlier (Fig. 4), and both theaters are essen-

7 / A Country Theater. Etching by Joseph Wright after the drawing by W. H. Pyne, 1789.

tially in the tradition of the conventional Restoration and eighteenth-century playhouse, though they display the kind of periodlessness and lack of definition that so often exists in basically amateur architecture. Both illustrations indicate clearly the rudimentary nature of auditoriums constructed to include only vitally essential features. In both theaters, for example, the stage appears to be flat and level with the auditorium floor, thus eliminating all but the most necessary construction. Likewise, the characteristic English apron or forestage has become nothing more than an open portion of the auditorium in front of the proscenium arch, and, since exits and entrances were perfectly possible from behind the stage wings, proscenium doors have been entirely eliminated. A crude proscenium balcony or window exists in the illustration of the fair booth, but the window has been moved to the face of the proscenium wall because of the absence of any doors leading onto the forestage.

At both theaters, however, the comparative luxury of a curtain was provided, and there was a token attempt to drape the proscenium arch in imitation of more elaborately decorated playhouses. Indeed, the theater booth in which the conjurer displays his tricks even boasts a motto of some sort painted on a panel above the stage, and both playhouses contain simplified versions of the great chandeliers that lighted the aprons of proper theaters.

The scenery displayed on the stage of the Country Theater is of some interest: for a performance (presumably of *Macbeth*) the manager has erected stationary wings that are haphazardly propped up from behind by crude wooden jacks and a litter of miscellaneous odds and ends. But there is not the slightest suggestion that the wings used on the stage of this crude little theater moved on and off in grooves like those found at better equipped playhouses. In the light of the whole character of the stage and auditorium this rather basic approach to the construction and rigging of the scenery is scarcely surprising—indeed, it is precisely what we might expect in a theater of the sort. Perhaps the only inconsistency behind the proscenium arch is the trap from which the witches are just appearing. One would not expect to find a trap door in a house that did not possess a raised stage floor. One suspects, in fact, that both witches and trap may have sprung full-blown from the artist's imagination in an attempt to provide an interesting focal point for his composition. It is possible, however, that the artist was literally correct and that the manager merely cut a large hole in the stage floor or employed a cellar entrance as a crude trap door.

Another English playhouse, the Winterslow House Theater (Fig. 8), in use for private performances as early as 1768, may provide some additional clues to the sort of building constructed by Levingston at Williamsburg. An oak-timbered barn, perhaps three or four hundred years old, the playhouse stands about a hundred yards from the site of the now vanished Winterslow House. The barn is rectangular in shape and is joined to a smaller structure on the north. The foundation, of flint and stone, rises to a height of about four feet; the upper portion of the building is of wood on a frame of oak. On the east side of the converted barn is a small entrance lobby with double doors; the interior of this lobby still contains some fragments of paneling up to a height of approximately five feet, with old lath and plaster above.

There is no conclusive evidence for the position of the stage in the Winterslow House Theater, except for the fact that a door was at some time cut into the north wall at a height of three or four feet above the floor. The door, which leads into the smaller barn, may have served as a stage-level entrance to dressing rooms located in the northernmost building. Thus, the chances are good that the stage was a raised platform—with or without a conventional proscenium arch and doors—at the north end of the barn. Such a conjecture is reinforced by the fact that the entrance lobby was placed off-center on the east face of the building and

8 / Winterslow House Theater.

that the northern portion of the barn is somewhat smaller than that on the south. A proscenium arch might well have been erected at a crossbeam located just north of the lobby door, and the whole south end of the structure devoted to audience seating. No trace of a raked floor has been located at either end of the structure, however, and in the absence of better evidence we must assume that such a refinement did not exist in the building.[12]

All in all, one imagines that the Winterslow House Theater was probably rather similar to the building shown in the 1789 print of the Country Theater. And one wonders if Levingston's theater was much better than either of these playhouses—buildings that seemingly stood midway between a fair booth and a proper theater. Perhaps, however, we do an injustice to Levingston and his playhouse by such a suggestion, for the evidence that the building was not a more or less conventional theater is scarcely conclusive. It was suggested earlier that the building may have been a simple version of a Restoration playhouse like Wren's Drury Lane—that it was conventionally divided into boxes, pit, and galleries and contained a raised stage with a raked floor and proscenium doors on a broad projecting apron. In such theaters the playgoer passed through the lobby and entered the auditorium by way of a pit passage or one of the flights of stairs that led to the boxes and galleries. Once inside the auditorium, the Restoration spectator found himself in a room the general features of which were close to those of English theaters of one hundred and fifty years later. His grandchildren—and indeed his great, great, grandchildren—would watch plays in theaters that were similar in many respects to the playhouses of the Restoration.

At Drury Lane, Wren designed an auditorium that was clearly in artificial perspective (Fig. 5). It has been suggested—although it is impossible to determine from Wren's longitudinal section—that the sides of the pit converged toward the stage, thus forming a house more or less fan-shaped in plan as well as section. Such a scheme was indeed typical of eighteenth-century playhouses, but recent scholarship points to an auditorium at Drury Lane that was straight-sided with curving banks of seats at the rear.[13]

The "pit" or main floor of early theaters was frequently sunk below ground level and sloped from the rear of the auditorium toward the stage. The seating in this area was nothing more than backless benches, much closer together than modern theater seats, and extending across the entire width of the pit from side wall to side wall. Today, it is almost inconceivable that a theater would be built without aisles of any sort, yet this was precisely the case in the Restoration and in much of the eighteenth century. In a sense, the passages that flanked the pit below the first tier of boxes were aisles since they allowed the spectator to pass downward toward the stage area. But it must be remembered that these passages were separated from the pit itself by solid walls, and that the spectator, when he had completed his walk from the lobby and entered the pit through a door near the stage, was forced to pass up to his seat by walking on the tops of the pit benches.

The location of boxes changed somewhat from the Restoration to the eighteenth century. Characteristically, the Restoration playhouse contained boxes only at the sides of the auditorium rather than around three sides of the pit, as in the case of theaters of the next century. In Wren's Drury Lane section, for example, there appear to be no subdivisions in either of the first two tiers of seats that rise at the rear of the auditorium on a line with the side boxes. The area on a line with the upper level of side boxes, in fact, was conventionally known as the Middle Gallery or Eighteenpenny Gallery. Occupying only the end of the auditorium, above the side box level, was the Upper or Twelvepenny Gallery, the cheapest seating in the house and the home of those very vocal spectators, the gallery gods.

The Restoration auditorium merged into the perspective stage setting in a way not possible in the modern proscenium playhouse. Wren's section of Drury Lane illustrates the point well, for we can see that the ten- or twelve-degree rake of the Drury Lane stage parallels the upward slope of the lower boxes, completing the artificial perspective of the auditorium and carrying it on to the apron and beyond the proscenium arch into the stagehouse. Proscenium doors, with balconies above, opened directly on the forestage. Wren's drawing of Drury Lane indicates that the theater possessed two pairs of entrances with their corresponding windows or balconies; but by the eighteenth century only a single pair was commonly used. This basic division of the stage into two parts, with doors and windows on the apron, was to last throughout most of the eighteenth century with only slight modifications, and indeed was to appear almost intact in some playhouses constructed in England and America well into the nineteenth century.

Levingston's playhouse may well have been arranged in this conventional way; and the only other building constructed as a permanent playhouse before the advent of the first professional managers, the Dock Street Theater in Charleston, was at least basically similar to proper English theaters of the period, for it contained the conventional box, pit, and gallery arrangement.[14] The first Charleston playhouse, located on the south side of Dock (or Queen) Street, was built in 1736 to house amateur players. In 1935 the theater site, on which the famous Planters' Hotel had later been erected, was selected as a government project of work relief. Apparently the basis of the selection rested with Charleston's well-intentioned but incorrect claim that the Dock Street Theater was the first American playhouse. A portion of the interior of the hotel was subsequently remodeled as a theater loosely based on English playhouses of the eighteenth century (Fig. 9).[15]

25

9 / Reconstruction of the Dock Street or Queen Street Theater, Charleston, South Carolina.

Later, the typically English division of the auditorium into some variation of the box, pit, and gallery formula seen at Dock Street was to become the American standard of theater construction; but the beginnings of the English playhouse in America were already in evidence well before the appearance of Murray and Kean and Lewis Hallam. The hall theater, the fair booth, and perhaps even a simple version of the conventional English playhouses were already known to colonists in the larger towns before the middle of the eighteenth century, and soon the professional players were to supplant these first crude essays in theater architecture with buildings based on those in which they had played in their native land.

II / Professional Beginnings

A large green curtain hung before the players until they were ready to begin, when, on the blast of a whistle, it was raised, and some of them appeared and commenced acting.
(Philip Schuyler, 1753)

There is reasonable doubt that the company of actors raised by Walter Murray and Thomas Kean deserved the title of professional players. Lewis Hallam, we know, spoke of them as "that Sett of Pretenders," although it is possible that he let professional jealousy influence his evaluation.[1] It is certain, in any case, that Murray and Kean did little to further the cause of theater building in the American colonies. The two managers, whose origins remain a mystery, probably had neither the money nor the technical knowledge to erect first-rate theater buildings.

They began their American tour in a temporary playhouse that was surely little better than those used by amateur performers in the thirties. Plumsted's warehouse, the building that Murray and Kean chose as a temporary home after their arrival in Philadelphia in 1749, was a large, rather unhandsome structure built of brick in Flemish bond with glazed headers, which stood near

10 / Plumsted's warehouse (at right). Detail from George Heap and Nicholas Scull, *An East Prospect of the City of Philadelphia*, 1754.

the docks in Water Street between Lombard and Pine.[2] The warehouse, which continued to stand on the waterfront as late as the middle of the nineteenth century, was pictured in Scull and Heap's *An East Prospect of the City of Philadelphia* of 1754 as a rather barren building with a steep gambrel roof (Fig. 10).

In 1750, Murray and Kean's troupe moved on to New York and announced that they had taken "a convenient Room for their Purpose, in one of the buildings lately belonging to the Hon. Rip Van Dam Esqr., deceased."[3] The building into which Murray and Kean moved was a former brewery located in Nassau Street. Perhaps the New Theater of 1732 was also located in the old brewery; however, T. Allston Brown suggests that the earlier

29

playhouse was in another building owned by Van Dam at the corner of Pearl Street and Maiden Lane.

For many years a description of the interior of Murray and Kean's Nassau Street playhouse has appeared in histories of American theater. Brown's description, however, was probably more the result of an overactive imagination and an inclination toward plagiarism than of any real evidence, for his account is frequently almost a word for word copy of a piece that appeared in William Dunlap's *History of the American Theatre*. The item Dunlap printed was taken from an account of the life of the English actor John Bernard. As a young man, Bernard played in a crude theater arranged by Jackson, the provincial manager, at the Black Bull Inn at Farnham. All in all, it is possible that the little theater in use at the Black Bull was indeed somewhat on the order of Murray and Kean's Nassau Street playhouse, and, for this reason, it seems worthwhile to set down the fragment from Bernard's life. Jackson, we are told:

engaged the largest room at the said Black Bull, suspended a collection of tatters along its middle for a curtain, erected a pair of paper screens, right hand and left, for wings; arranged four candles in front of said wings, to divide said wings from the orchestra (the fiddlers' chairs being the legitimate division of the orchestra from the pit); and with all the spare benches of the inn to form boxes, and a hoop suspended from the ceiling (perforated with a dozen nails to receive as many tallow candles) to suggest the idea of a chandelier; he had embellished what he called a theatre. The scenery consisted of two drops . . . the inside of a house and the outside of a house. The first was a kitchen, with all its implements; by the simple introduction of two chairs and a table, this was constituted a gentleman's parlour; and, in the further presence of a crimson-cushioned yellow-legged elbow-chair, with a banner behind and stool in front, was elevated into a royal hall of audience. The other drop (which I have termed the outside of a house) presented on its surface two houses peeping in at the sides, a hill, a wood, a stream, a bridge, and a distant plain.[4]

If the Nassau Street Theater did begin its existence as such a primitive structure, it would appear that some changes took place shortly to bring it more in line with English theaters of the time. The advertisement for the opening of the house does not mention boxes of any sort; but a card inserted in the newspapers in 1751 indicates that for a performance in the theater there were "161 pit tickets, 10 Boxes, and 121 Gallery Tickets, printed in all."[5] Permanent boxes may have been installed at this time or, as Joseph Ireland suggested, the managers may have made use of some variation of the common English custom of railing off a portion of the pit as temporary boxes.[6] Probably the Nassau Street Theater was little if any improvement on the earlier theater in William Plumsted's warehouse—and it is likely that neither playhouse represented any substantial improvement over the amateur houses in use earlier in the century.

At least some sign of progress is to be seen with the first building actually constructed as a playhouse after the beginning of the so-called professional period of American theater. Yet one has serious doubts that this theater, the second Williamsburg playhouse, constructed in 1751 for Murray and Kean, owed much to either the London or provincial houses of the time. The building originally stood on two lots on the east side of Eastern or Waller Street, not far from the Capitol. The foundations have not been located, but the supposition that it was a rather crude wooden affair seems to be demonstrated by the scanty information that survives. It is plain that there was no time to erect an elaborate house, for the theater took only two months to construct; and, indeed, we know that the managers themselves had little or no part in its design or execution since the building was erected for them before they arrived in Williamsburg.[7]

If any doubt remains about the quality of the second Williamsburg theater, we have only to look ahead to the period in which the playhouse was occupied by the somewhat more affluent and better-trained Hallam company. When Lewis Hallam took over the building, he "enlarged it" and "entirely altered the Play-House at *Williamsburg* to a regular Theatre, fit for the Reception of Ladies and Gentlemen."[8] Hallam's decision to enlarge the building suggests that the structure in its earliest form was too small to accommodate a profitable number of spectators and too uncomfortable for the proper entertainment of the Williamsburg gentry. And—although the evidence of a single word should not be considered conclusive—it might be noted that Hallam spoke of having converted the building to a *regular* theater. Precisely what changes he made in the fabric of the playhouse are not known; but it is certain that the earliest building did contain at least a simple division into boxes, pit, and gallery, and that the remodeling by Hallam maintained this division, although in a less primitive form.

When Murray and Kean abandoned the Williamsburg playhouse in November 1751, they moved on to Norfolk. Here they presented a play at a temporary theater in "Capt. Newton's Great Room," presumably setting up a rough stage much like that used by the earlier amateur players.[9] Throughout the months that followed they played on an improvised stage at the courthouse in Tappahannock, and in a building at Fredericksburg that the young George Washington referred to in his ledger as "the playhouse."[10]

An incredible amount of confusion has always surrounded the next theater occupied by Murray and Kean in 1752. Dunlap remarked with complete conviction that "Annapolis has the honour of having raised the first temple to the Muses" in the American colonies.[11] But there is reasonable doubt that Murray and Kean raised a temple of any sort in Annapolis in that year. It is much more likely that they played in a converted warehouse that tradition places on Duke of Gloucester Street. Unfortunately, our knowledge of the managers' contribution to the building consists only of the fact that they thoughtfully "raised a Porch at the Door that will keep out the inclemency of the weather."[12]

After a sojourn at the town of Chester, Maryland, the troupe moved on to Upper Marlborough, where they performed in the "New Theatre," a building that contained only a pit and gallery. It may well be that the New Theater at Upper Marlborough was the "neat convenient tobacco-house, well fitted up for the purpose" that was used by the later manager, David Douglass, during his salad days in the colonies.[13] The managers had announced that they would also play at Piscataway and Port Tobacco, and perhaps they did, although no further record of the company's activities remains. Murray and Kean disappeared from the American theater. Their contribution to the theater architecture of the American colonies was admittedly a small one. Probably the theaters that they outfitted in Philadelphia, New York, Williamsburg, and in a number of sleepy southern villages were little more advanced than the earlier amateur buildings. It remained for Lewis Hallam—son of a theatrical family known to audiences at both Covent Garden and the booths of Bartholomew Fair—to begin the real history of English theater architecture in America.

On June 2, 1752, the *Charming Sally,* carrying Hallam and his company, dropped anchor at Yorktown. Within a few days the manager had arrived at Williamsburg, perhaps lured by the fact that Murray and Kean's playhouse already existed in the town. Hallam purchased the theater building from Alexander Finnie, keeper of the Raleigh Tavern, for £150 10s., and set about the creation of his "regular Theatre."[14] The playhouse, after Hal-

11 / Georgian theater, Richmond, Yorkshire, 1788. View of the auditorium from the stage.

lam's remodeling, probably resembled the simplest sort of provincial theater building. Whether it could claim any particular architectural or technical merit seems doubtful, but it was undeniably a substantial improvement over the building originally constructed for Murray and Kean.

As well as boxes, a pit, and a gallery, the remodeled theater contained "balconies" of some sort.[15] The location of these balconies is not known; however, two possibilities for their placement in the building at once suggest themselves. Above the proscenium doors of most eighteenth-century theaters of any pretentions there continued to be placed the windows or balconies seen in Restoration playhouses. Commonly these balconies were employed in the action of the play. But in England, when not needed by the players, the spaces were frequently sold to spec-

12 / Georgian theater, Richmond, Yorkshire, 1788. View of the stage from the auditorium.

tators, and it is very likely that just such an arrangement was in effect in Hallam's Williamsburg playhouse.

Another possibility is also plausible. It is likely that Murray and Kean's theater possessed only a single row of boxes at the rear of the auditorium, beneath the gallery. Hallam's alteration of the theater may have resulted in the construction of side boxes. Let us assume for the moment that this was the case. Small English playhouses like that at Richmond, Yorkshire (Figs. 11, 12, 13), contained only a single tier of boxes around the periphery of the pit rather than two or more tiers as in more important theaters. At Richmond and other theaters of its type the area above the side boxes was open space, with or without fixed benches, and totally lacking partitions of any sort. At many English houses the areas so arranged were called the slips—spaces that were, strictly

13 / Georgian theater, Richmond, Yorkshire, 1788. View of the stage and auditorium from a side box.

speaking, neither boxes nor galleries—and it is possible that the second Williamsburg playhouse contained areas of this sort that Hallam designated balconies.

Another item connected with the remodeling of the theater is perhaps worth mentioning since it appears many times in both English and American accounts of eighteenth-century playhouses. When Hallam altered the Williamsburg theater he at least partially "lined" the house. Precisely what Hallam meant by lining is not known; but from the context in which the word was most commonly used in the eighteenth century, it is probable that he meant nothing more than the process of plastering or in some other way finishing the inner surface of the theater's walls to insulate the house better, give it a somewhat more genteel appearance, and provide some sort of acoustical aid to the actor. It may be that the word as Hallam used it also applied to the ceiling as well as the walls of the theater. It is certain, in any event, that at least one early American playhouse stood in sore need of such treatment, for when Nancy Hallam sang at Annapolis in 1770, a choleric critic deplored the "Ruggedness of the Roof" and its unfortunate effect upon the "Musick of her Tongue."[16]

If William Dunlap is to be believed, the house after its alteration still contained no proper orchestra pit or only a very small one, for he tells us that the Hallam company performed at Williamsburg with only a harpsichord for accompaniment.[17] It is also likely that the manager's alterations represented no very high order of carpentry, or that some of Hallam's improvements were destroyed by a fire that Dunlap mentions, for in the theater's last years gallery and balcony tickets appear not to have been sold.[18]

It is assumed that the Williamsburg theater during the tenure of Lewis Hallam possessed a sloping pit floor of some sort. The relatively sophisticated division of the house into four parts suggests that such a comparative nonessential as a raked floor was possible and even likely. Yet there is not any absolute evidence of a raked floor in any American theater for many years to come. This does not mean that such floors did not exist: they were almost certainly found in the theaters of David Douglass if not in Hallam's houses. But like so many of the physical details of the eighteenth-century American playhouse, no one cared sufficiently to record the fact.

But the record is not always totally barren. There are, for example, some indications of the nature of the stage and equipment in use at the second Williamsburg playhouse during the Hallam period. As it was first constructed for Murray and Kean, the playhouse at Williamsburg probably possessed only a small stage and little scenery or equipment of any real merit. Under the management of Lewis Hallam, however, it is likely that the stage as well as the auditorium was enlarged. The manager, in all events, spoke of the remodeled house as being well adapted to the performances of the company.[19] Perhaps this boast of Hallam's ought to be taken with a grain of salt; but whatever the size of his stage, it is quite clear that it was better furnished than those previously in use in the colonies. On June 12, 1752, a card in the *Virginia Gazette* informed the public of an innovation of some significance. The Company of Comedians from London was shortly to arrive in Williamsburg, and "the Scenes, Cloaths and Decorations are all entirely new, extremely rich, and finished in the highest Taste, the Scenes being painted by the best Hands in *London,* are excell'd by none in Beauty and Elegance, so that the Ladies and Gentlemen may depend on being entertain'd in as polite a Manner as at the Theatres in London." Once again it would appear that Hallam's penchant for superlatives had got the better of him: there could literally have been no comparison between the scenery he imported and that used at Drury Lane and Covent Garden. Yet, by stretching the point a little, he may have been reporting the facts with a fair degree of fidelity, for it is likely that the scenery had come from the insignificant London theater in Goodman's Fields run by Hallam's brother.[20] Presumably the scenes had been brought to America by Hallam himself on the *Charming Sally,* but it is doubtful that they were either very good or very new. Probably they consisted of nothing more than a few pairs of stock wings and a backdrop or two in the manner of Jackson's Black Bull settings or the crude scenery sketched later in the century by John Durang (see Figs. 14 and 15), actor, dancer, scene painter, and father of Charles Durang, the historian of the Philadelphia stage.

Whatever the quality of the settings that Hallam employed at his theater, one fact is certain: they were the first English scenes

14 / John Durang in Character of the Dwarf Metamorphosed. Water-color by John Durang, c. 1800.

15 / John Durang in Character of a Hornpipe. Watercolor by John
Durang, c. 1800.

to be used on the American stage. Before the arrival of the London company almost no attention was paid to the matter of scenery; Levingston, in fact, slights the whole question by referring only to "Cloaths Musick & other Necessaries required for Acting the said Plays."[21] But as well as better scenery, Hallam and his troupe could claim several other refinements that had not appeared at earlier colonial theaters. As in the London and provincial houses of the time, the stage at Hallam's theater contained a row of spikes that separated players and audience, and almost certainly a conventional forestage with proscenium doors and windows.[22] It is likely that if footlights of any sort existed at the second Williamsburg playhouse, they were nothing more than candles set down at intervals along the front of the apron in reflectors of some sort. The shield that kept the light of the candles from the eyes of the spectators may have been nothing more than a long plank set on edge at the very front of the forestage; however, it is not unlikely that each candle was fitted with a separate masking device. At least the possibility of such a scheme exists, for in 1953 a curious object that resembles a footlight shield was discovered in the attic of the St. George Tucker house at Williamsburg (Fig. 16). It may be that the object is indeed a footlight, used at either the first or second Williamsburg playhouse, since it is of eighteenth-century origin. It is constructed, however, of light wood or cardboard covered with handmade linen cloth rather than of metal, which suggests a pattern rather than an actual footlight shield. Or it may have had some other, quite domestic purpose. But the so-called footlight is painted green, the traditional color for playhouse interiors, and it is possible that it may have contained a separate tin sconce that protected the fabric from the candle flame. However doubtful the evidence, it is the only clue to the possible nature of the stage lighting in use at Williamsburg during the Hallam period.[23]

16 / Supposed
footlight
found at
Williamsburg,
Virginia.

The later record of the Hallam theater becomes, at the same
time, both increasingly complex and annoyingly vague. But the
facts seem to indicate that sometime after its tenancy by the
Hallam company, the theater was moved across Waller Street to
a lot in the Capitol Square. By 1787 the building had disappeared altogether and bricks, presumably from the foundation
of the theater, were sold to a local mason.[24]

Following their departure from Williamsburg, Hallam and his
troupe played at theaters in New York, Philadelphia, and Charleston.[25] At Philadelphia, Plumsted's warehouse was once again

put into service. It is apparent that Hallam improved the building somewhat, adding boxes to the house and presumably making at least some attempt to decorate the interior. Dunlap tells us that "remains or traces of scenic decoration" existed at Plumsted's warehouse long after it ceased to be used as a theater building.[26] Unfortunately, it is not clear whether Dunlap was referring to decoration on the walls of the auditorium or to fragments of wings and backdrops that lay abandoned in the old theater. But it is likely that Hallam did, in fact, attempt to remove a bit of the barrenness of the warehouse by adding some decorative features, for we know that above the proscenium arch he inscribed the words *Totus Mundus agit Histrionem* in imitation of the motto above the stage at Drury Lane. Dunlap, in fact, tells us that the motto was a permanent feature of all colonial playhouses.[27] It is doubtful that this was actually the case, but the Latin words—commonly translated as "The whole world acts the player"—appeared at several houses before the Revolution.[28]

Before leaving for Philadelphia, Hallam had set up a theater in the Nassau Street building formerly used by Murray and Kean as a New York playhouse. Hallam's reaction to the building shows the manager's continuing dissatisfaction with the makeshift theaters in which he was forced to perform. In July of 1753, he rather peevishly addressed himself to the people of the city, pointing out that he had been promised a "very fine Play-house Building."[29] Instead, of course, he was forced to work in the converted brewery that had recently belonged to the estate of Rip Van Dam. By September, however, the *Post-Boy* reported that "the Company of Comedians . . . have built a very fine, large and commodious Theatre in the place where the old One Stood."[30] How truthfully the *Post-Boy* recorded the glories of the new playhouse we do not know, but it was clearly a landmark of American theater architecture. It was the first playhouse that

43

Hallam built in the colonies, and probably the first colonial build-ing to be literally based on the theaters of England. It may have owed something to the overall design of one of the Patent theaters or a provincial playhouse, and there is every reason to believe that it borrowed to some extent from the obscure London theater that had been managed by Hallam's brother, the New Wells Theater, Goodman's Fields. All in all, one imagines that the new Nassau Street Theater was probably not "fine, large and commodious" except in comparison to what had come before, but it did mark the real beginnings of theater architecture in America.

Since the Nassau Street Theater was the first American play-house designed with the needs of a professional company in mind, its technical aspects undoubtedly signaled an improvement over anything previously seen in the colonies. Presumably the stage was conventionally divided, and equipped with at least one stan-dard item of English theater furniture. In 1753, Philip Schuyler saw at the playhouse "a large green curtain [that] hung before the players until they were ready to begin."[31] Schuyler's chance remark is of some interest, for the green curtain was to remain standard equipment in American playhouses throughout much of the eighteenth century.

During the Restoration the green curtain commonly rose after the prologue was delivered on the forestage and did not descend again until after the epilogue was spoken. Montague Summers asserts, however, that by the middle of the eighteenth century a second curtain was usually lowered to make act divisions.[32] Whether an additional curtain of this sort was introduced in colo-nial America is not known; but it is clear, in any case, that the typical green front curtain used on American stages was of the roller variety. Roller curtains of a similar type are still frequently constructed (although of canvas rather than baize) for revivals of nineteenth-century melodramas, and embellished with local scenes and comic advertisements. As in the eighteenth century,

44

such curtains are usually rigged with the actual roller at the bottom, although some English drops contained a top roller much in the manner of a modern window shade.[33] The great virtues of a roller curtain, from the manager's point of view, lay in the essential simplicity of its construction and rigging, the ease with which it could be stored or moved from place to place, and the fact that it required only a few scant inches of space above the proscenium arch. It is virtually certain that the first managers carried such a square of green baize from theater to theater, perhaps mounted on a roller that was nothing more than a log from which the bark was removed. We can only guess at the nature of the other items of stage furniture used at the second Nassau Street playhouse, although it is probably safe to suggest that the scenery used in the theater was that seen previously at Williamsburg. Beyond these few scraps of information there is little more to record. When Hallam left New York for Philadelphia in March 1754, he sold the building for the equivalent of $1,250 to a society of German Calvinists who converted the theater into a church, later razing the building and erecting another church on the site.[34]

Two years after the sale of the theater, Hallam died, the victim of an epidemic of yellow fever that swept the island of Jamaica. Hallam's death marked the end of an era. Under his management the first tentative attempts to establish the English theater building in the colonies had taken place. The company that formed in Jamaica under David Douglass and his bride, Lewis Hallam's widow, was to carry the whole process a step further; for although the buildings that Douglass erected to house his company were of somewhat doubtful merit when considered as architecture, they clearly represented the acceptance of the English playhouse as the theater of the American colonies.

III / The Rise of David Douglass

To You, our Friends, rais'd by whose bounteous Hands,
This rude, and yet unpolish'd Fabrick stands;
Great is the Debt of Gratitude we owe . . .
(David Douglass, 1771)

In Jamaica David Douglass played in a theater in Harbour Street that had been converted from a government warehouse; after his arrival on the mainland, he performed in a former sail loft on Cruger's Wharf in New York.[1] By 1759, however, Douglass had erected his own theater at Vernon and South Streets in Southwark, just outside the Philadelphia city limits. The structure was considered large for its time, and cost "£300 & upwards" to erect, no great sum, but a substantial advance over the £150 10s. that Hallam had expended for Murray and Kean's theater and two lots in Williamsburg.[2] This "Theatre on Society Hill," which was built and furnished by two men with the improbable names of Alexander Alexander and William Williams, was constructed of wood. It was later remodeled into three dwelling houses, or was pulled down and some of its material used in the construction of three houses erected on the theater site. The houses, which were still standing a few years ago, contained parts of a brick wall traditionally believed to have been the early theater's proscenium arch. But the fact that the playhouse was never used after 1759 suggests it was little more than a temporary theater building, with little if any brick construction in its fabric.[3]

Though Society Hill was a building of somewhat dubious merit, the scenery it contained was presumably the finest ever seen in the colonies. The old scenery that Hallam had brought from England must have been largely abandoned in Jamaica, for Douglass purchased a complete stock of new scenes for the opening of the playhouse on Society Hill. The price that the painter, William Williams, received is of some interest, for it amounted to a very substantial outlay, especially when considered in the light of the cost of the theater building itself. Society Hill cost something over £300, and "a new set of scenes for the said theatre" about £100, an unusually high amount at first glance.[4] But it should be noted that Douglass' peripatetic company undoubtedly transported the same stock scenes to every house it played, thus making good use of Douglass' original expenditure. By 1761 Douglass claimed that he had invested some £400 in costumes and scenery.[5] Although the manager may have been exaggerating his expenses, it is quite possible that in two years he had almost doubled his store of backdrops and wings as the number of his theaters increased.

It seems likely that Douglass developed some sort of master plan for a theater that he carried with him from place to place, for two of his later playhouses resemble each other in many important ways. Although such a plan may have been little more than a series of crude drawings and sketches of his own conception, it was undoubtedly based on English playhouses of the time. It is likely that Douglass also had in his possession plans of specific English houses, as well as sketches or prints of their exteriors, and that these materials substantially influenced the Society Hill playhouse. Unfortunately, it is impossible to say which buildings he may have used as models for his American theaters.

There is no information relating Douglass' next playhouse, constructed at Annapolis in 1760, to English sources or to the earlier theater on Society Hill at Philadelphia; the Annapolis structure is known only as a wooden building, "on a small scale and inconveniently located."[6] His next theater, erected at Newport, Rhode

Island, in 1761, remains almost equally obscure. It is clear that the building "stood on a lot on the north of that part of town called Easton's Point, near Dyer's Gate." Beyond this fact we know only that the theater was the already traditional "slight wooden structure, hastily erected."[7]

In the same year that he built the Newport playhouse, Douglass constructed a new theater in New York, the Beekman Street or Chapel Street Theater. Although it was almost certainly better than the playhouses at Newport and Annapolis, the New York theater was evidently flimsy, for it was almost totally destroyed by a mob in one night during the course of a theater riot in 1766.[8] An advertisement of 1764 indicated that the playhouse was for rent and that it was "very convenient for a Store, being upwards of 90 feet in Length, nigh 40 feet wide."[9] This is the first positive set of playhouse dimensions known after the arrival of the English companies in America, and the large size of the structure suggests that contemporary statements that the building seated 352 spectators and cost more than £650 are quite reasonable.[10]

The interior of the Chapel Street Theater is comparatively well documented for so early a building and provides some information of real significance concerning the arrangement of boxes, pit, and gallery in the earliest professional playhouses. The theater was, as we know, more than 90 feet long and something less than 40 feet in width, with an auditorium that seated 146 in the boxes, 116 in the pit, and 90 in the gallery. Presumably the pit floor in so large a house was sloped from the rear of the auditorium to the stage; and it is known that there were at least two tiers of side boxes flanking the pit as well as boxes on the stage itself.[11] An advertisement that Douglass inserted in the New York *Mercury,* March 8, 1762, would appear to indicate that the upper tier of boxes originally took the form of slips, for on that date the manager announced: "There are Partitions made to divide the side Boxes, from one another, and thereby render them more commodious for select company." Probably the building possessed pit passages, although their presence is never mentioned in early accounts. If such passages did exist they were almost certainly damp, narrow, and airless corridors, sunk below ground level and certain death traps in case of a fire. The Richmond, Surrey, playhouse possessed precisely such a nightmare passage to the pit, and when the early nineteenth-century playhouse in the American city of the same name burned in 1811, it was estimated that a theater of the sort could not be emptied in less than an hour.[12]

Entrance to the gallery of a theater like that in Chapel Street was by a narrow and tortuous flight of stairs that rose from a small lobby, containing a pay booth, near the front of the building. Entrance to the lower boxes may have been through a narrow corridor onto which the doors of the various boxes opened, but it is more likely in this case that the lower box partitions stopped short of the side walls of the theater, allowing a narrow space for passage from the lobby to the boxes nearest the front of the auditorium.

The upper boxes (or slips) at Chapel Street were entered in a somewhat curious way. On December 31, 1761, the *Post-Boy* carried a card announcing: "It will be taken as a particular Favour if no Gentleman will be offended that he is absolutely denied Admittance at the Stage Door, unless he has secured himself a place in the Stage or Upper Boxes." That the stage boxes could only have been entered from behind the scenes seems logical enough, but to require the same procedure of the spectators in the upper boxes appears strange at first. Yet it was not uncommon: the *Maryland Gazette* (Annapolis) for February 16, 1769, informed the public that "upper boxes are now preparing, the Passage to which must be from the stage."

Probably entrance to the upper boxes or slips from backstage was the result of increased need for seating space in the auditorium. If such a theater were altered to provide slips or upper boxes there were probably only two means of making the altera-

49

tion without resorting to extensive remodeling. On the one hand, the gallery stairs might be used to reach the top boxes; but social distinctions being what they were in the eighteenth century, it seems unlikely that holders of box tickets would have cared to enter the theater with the gods and goddesses of the gallery when another alternative could be provided. On the other hand, entrance was quite possible from behind the scenes if doors were cut into the proscenium wall at the upper box level and flights of stairs added in the wings. Thus a separate entrance, however inconvenient, would have been provided for the upper boxes from the stage door, and the more favored patrons would have been spared association with the footmen and chambermaids nearby. Further to discourage fraternization—as well as attempts to gain a box seat without additional cost—at least one early theater contained a wicked row of metal spikes between the gallery and the upper boxes, and perhaps a similar barrier between lower boxes and pit.[13]

We have no idea whether the stage at Chapel Street was fitted out like those of the better English provincial theaters of the middle eighteenth century. It is likely, however, that Douglass' playhouse in Chapel Street contained at least the basic equipment found in the better class of minor British theaters. If this was indeed the case, Chapel Street possessed at least a simple version of the conventional English groove system for shifting scenery. The technical details of this system of scene shifting properly belong later; suffice it to say here that the lower grooves and the wings that they contained would have taken up considerable offstage space to the left and right of the proscenium opening. When one considers that the stagehouse also contained packs of wings not in use at the moment, the properties employed in the play being performed, the miscellaneous collection of worn-out equipment invariably found backstage at any theater, and flights of stairs to the upper boxes, it is apparent that there was precious little unused space behind the proscenium arch. Thus Douglass' frequent pleas to the auditors to remain in their own part of the house were well founded, if not always honored by the beaux of the period.[14]

In spite of its defects, the Chapel Street Theater was surely Douglass' most elaborate theater building until the construction of the John Street and Southwark playhouses in the later 1760's. It was almost certainly a better building than the earlier theater on Society Hill at Philadelphia, and probably far superior to the Charleston playhouse he erected in Queen Street in 1762, although the dimensions of the theater at Charleston (35 feet by 75 feet) indicate that it was not unusually small.[15] One imagines that all three buildings were run-of-the-mill theaters, roughly comparable to many of the less important provincial playhouses that were being constructed in England at mid-century. Douglass' lesser efforts were surely primitive indeed. The theaters at Annapolis and Newport we know to have been shabby structures; and the playhouse that Douglass erected at Providence in 1762 was a crude building later described as little better than a barn.[16]

The Philadelphia, New York, and perhaps the Charleston playhouses represented Douglass' best efforts as theater designer for the simple reason that the largest and best theater buildings were required in these comparatively large and relatively cosmopolitan towns. Annapolis, Newport, and Providence represented the "second line" on the Douglass circuit—towns in which a theater building was required, but in which it was neither necessary nor wise to construct theaters of any real permanence. Such a plan of expansion was to become the common pattern for American theater building in the colonial period. Douglass erected theaters wherever there seemed the chance of a reasonable community response. The fortunes of these buildings followed the fortunes of the towns in which they stood. As support increased, the old playhouses were sold or razed and new and better buildings erected. And once his position was established in any town, Douglass moved on to other, smaller towns, following the theatrical frontier and repeating his whole scheme of expansion once again.

IV / The Southwark and John Street

It was principally of wood; an unsightly object, painted red.
(William Dunlap, on the John Street Theater)

As David Douglass grew more prosperous during the late 1760's the opportunity for architectural permanence, if not architectural elegance, had at last arrived. A case in point is the famous Southwark Theater, erected just outside the city limits of Philadelphia in 1766. That the building was at least solidly built is attested by the fact that it was in use for over half a century after its construction.[1] It cost more than twice as much as Douglass' earlier Philadelphia playhouse on Society Hill, and was 50 feet wide, 95 feet long.[2] A reconstruction by Charles Durang (Fig. 17) indicates that the theater, which stood in Cedar Street between Fourth and Fifth Streets, was two and one half stories high, with the foundation and first story of brick and the second of wood. Durang's sketch is badly out of scale, but it clearly shows that the front of the building on the south side of Cedar Street was graced with a trio of round-headed windows. Actually, these were ordinary rectangular openings "painted in the Venetian [Palladian] style."[3] A cupola topped the building. It may be that the cupola

17 / Conjectural reconstruction of the Southwark Theater, in 1766, based on the research of Charles Durang, 1884.

served a practical as well as a decorative function. In 1767 it was announced that "there are some alterations made in the House, in order to render it Cool."[4] Perhaps the curious ogee-roofed cupola contained ventilators of some sort to bring fresh air into the auditorium; such an arrangement appears to have been in use at Douglass' later John Street Theater.

It is clear that the house was poorly insulated if, indeed, it was insulated at all, for complaints about both excessive summer heat and winter cold were recorded. One wonders just how much shelter from the elements the Southwark did provide. Durang, for example, suggests that the theater was "built in too great a hurry," and that it "leaked a good deal, and it was scarcely ever dry."[5] It is also apparent that the playhouse was almost impossible to enter in wet weather, for prior to 1790, when a brick sidewalk was built near the theater, playgoers approached it over an improvised walk constructed of planks.[6]

All in all, the contemporary criticism that the Southwark was "an ugly, ill-contrived affair" seems manifestly true, although it is well to remember that it was probably the first really substantial theater building the colonists had seen and the largest in America up to that time. One other point is interesting in relation to the Southwark. Earlier it was suggested that Douglass probably developed some master plan for construction of theater buildings in the colonies: the Southwark represents the first evidence that such a hypothesis is true, for the plan of that theater was used as the basis of New York's John Street Theater, constructed the next year.[7]

Very little is known about the exterior of the John Street Theater, although it seems likely that it differed in no significant way from Philadelphia's Southwark. The playhouse in John Street, in fact, appears to have had only one feature not seen in the Philadelphia theater, a long covered walkway that led from the street to the theater door. Jonathan's famous speech from Royall Tyler's play *The Contrast* tells part of the story. "I saw," said Jonathan, "a great crowd of folks going into a long entry, that had lantherns over the door."[8] Dunlap tells us that the theater "was about 60 feet back from the street, having a covered way of rough wooden material from the pavement to the doors."[9]

Beyond this fact little is known about the exterior of the theater in John Street except that, like the Southwark, "it was principally of wood; an unsightly object, painted red," and that it stood on the north side of the street,[10] It also seems likely that John Street, like the Southwark, was crowned with a cupola to house a ventilating system, for in 1793 a wind sail was erected on the theater, and in June of 1795 it was announced that the ventilator would be opened at the top of the house in order to render the auditorium cool.[11]

With Philadelphia's Southwark and New York's John Street theaters—whatever their crudities—the design of the American playhouse probably reached its highest point before the closing of the theaters in 1774. The Southwark, in any case, probably differed little from many respectable but unimpressive town theaters across the Atlantic. A mysterious visitor to the playhouse, known only as "Lang Syne," saw the Southwark some twenty years after its construction and recorded a helpful if not precisely glowing description of it: "The building, compared with the new houses, was an ugly, ill-contrived affair outside and inside. The stage lighted by plain oil lamps without glasses. The view from the boxes was intercepted by large square wooden pillars supporting the upper tier and roof. It was contended by many, at the time, that the front bench in the gallery was the best seat for a fair view of the whole stage.[12]

Lang Syne's critique of the house, and the other accounts that have survived, provide a fair picture of the theater's interior. The Southwark possessed the standard arrangement of boxes, pit, and gallery, pit passages and a stage fronted by a row of iron spikes.[13] In spite of the ventilating devices used at John Street and the Southwark, one imagines that the buildings were incredibly hot during the summer months, and it is likely that they were equally uncomfortable during the winter season. At least token attempts were made to warm the playhouses, however, for one John Aymer received the sum of £1 7s. "for three nights attendance the lamps and fires below the stage."[14] It is likely that Douglass, like his predecessor, also allowed small foot stoves to be carried into some

55

parts of his theater in spite of the hazard of fire.[15] One wonders why, in the presence of a hundred different open flames in stoves and lighting equipment, there were not more serious fires in these early wooden playhouses. Lang Syne, for example, indicates that the stage at the Southwark was "lighted by plain oil lamps without glasses"—a virtual invitation to holocaust.

The use of these oil lamps on the stage provides a possible clue to lighting in other parts of the house. Late in the century a patent lamp, employing the Argand burner for oil, with a cylindrical wick and glass chimney, was widely used in English theaters, reducing somewhat the danger of fire. During the early period of the John Street and Southwark playhouses, however, only the common oil lamp was available. If such lamps were used on the stage it is highly likely that they also appeared elsewhere, for they were even cheaper than ordinary tallow candles. Probably, as in some British theaters, these evil-smelling objects were the only source of light in the gallery and pit passages. The spectators in pit and boxes, however, were provided with more and better light than the servants who occupied the gallery above. In many British theaters of the time chandeliers were suspended from the ceiling over the forestage and, in some cases, from the box ceilings as well. Most playhouses seem also to have been provided with candle brackets (or "branches" as they were often called) on the box fronts and on the stage itself (Fig. 18).

Perhaps the earliest reference to the use of candles in an American playhouse comes from David Douglass' account of his expenses for a benefit performance of *Othello* at Chapel Street in 1762. Among the expenditures of the evening we find: "To Candles, 26 lbs. Spermacete at 3s. 6 and 14 lb. Tallow at 12d. £5 5s 0d."[16] This same mixture of tallow and spermaceti candles was known to have been used at John Street, and probably was employed in most American theaters until the Argand lamp became common. As Douglass' account clearly shows, the spermaceti

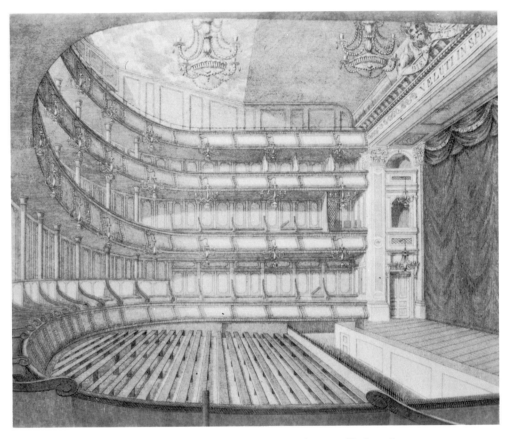

18 / The enlarged Covent Garden in 1794. Note the candle brackets on the stage and box fronts.

candle was by far the superior article: it burned better and dripped substantially less than the ordinary tallow candle dipped from animal fat. Usually the spermaceti candle was used to light the stage and forestage areas, with the cheaper tallow candles serving in the branches around the edge of the pit and in whatever sconces the management saw fit to place within the boxes.

There is only one other clue to the nature of the interior of the Southwark—a single line from Durang that may or may not be based on actual fact. In describing the old playhouse he speaks of "the dingy-papered boxes" in the auditorium.[17] Whether Durang was merely generalizing about an eighteenth-century custom or speaking with direct reference to the house is not known. Seemingly the earliest American playhouses were not finished on the inside; however, by the period of the Southwark and John Street, it is likely that the better houses were plastered or finished in some other regular way. If the auditoriums of the 1760's and 1770's followed standard British practice in interior decoration (as they apparently did in other matters), the appearance of box, pit, and gallery was stereotyped to a high degree. Later British and American playhouses of the eighteenth century seem to have displayed an increasing individuality in their interior color and appointments, but many of the houses erected before the last years of the century appear to have possessed auditoriums that conformed to a single decorative convention. Frequently, the English auditorium of the period was painted green: at Drury Lane in 1783, for example, the painting was somewhat cryptically described as "a very faint kind of pea green or rather a greenish colour."[18] The uppermost boxes in such theaters were usually painted to match the auditorium trim and, over the years, became known in theater parlance as "Green Boxes" no matter what their color. The lower tiers were frequently hung with crimson moreen or, in lesser houses, lined with red paper. Such a scheme of papering the boxes in imitation of moreen hangings may well have

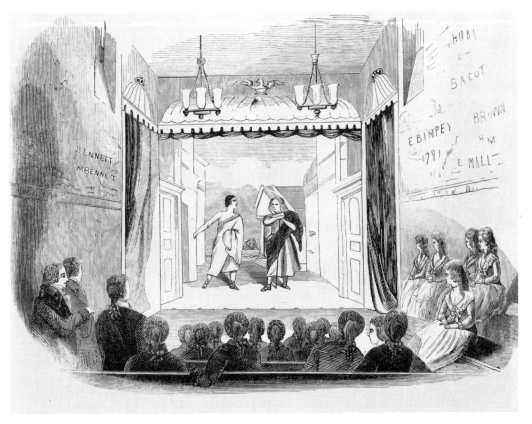

19 / Spurious view of the interior of the John Street Theater, c. 1870.

been used at the Southwark and in Douglass' other important houses.

The chances are good that all of Douglass' better theaters generally resembled one another in matters of interior arrangement and decoration. In spite of the well known prints of the John Street Theater's interior (Figs. 19 and 20), it is likely that its auditorium, like its exterior, was basically copied from the earlier

59

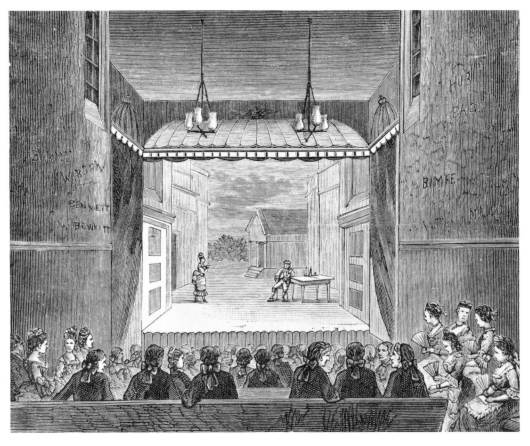

20 / Spurious view of the interior of the John Street Theater, c. 1870.

Southwark. These prints, which have appeared in many modern histories of the American theater, show a long, narrow, and extraordinarily ugly room of no great height, without conventional side boxes of any sort. The scene on the stage features, in one case, actors wrapped in what appear to be bed sheets and, in another, an eighteenth-century actress with a suspiciously Victorian bustle. The prints, of course, are a hoax, probably first perpetrated in the 1870's and evidently based on Westminster school plays of the period.[19] The John Street Theater—however inadequate—was almost certainly not so dismal a playhouse as these widely published prints have led us to believe.

By the period of the John Street and Southwark Theaters the stage and the equipment it contained were obviously far more elaborate than anything previously seen in the colonies. This is not to suggest that any of the theaters constructed in America just before the Revolution contained much behind their proscenium arches that was of an extraordinarily high order, but it is clear that by the middle and late sixties the better colonial stages had begun to compare favorably with those in many of the smaller English houses. As early as 1766 Douglass had gone back to England and returned with "a most excellent set of scenes done by Mr. Doll [Nicholas Thomas Dall] principal scene-painter to Covent Garden House."[20] The manager repeated his order in 1771, once again receiving a new stock of scenery from Dall.[21] A year later, still another set of scenes made its appearance, this time from the brush of John Inigo Richards, the London designer who, in later years, was to send to America the plans of Philadelphia's Chestnut Street Theater.[22] It is apparent that Douglass was rapidly building up his store of scenes and, perhaps for the first time, equipping the stage of each theater on his circuit in order to avoid the necessity of moving his sets from place to place. It is clear, too, that he now possessed the money to hire first-rate London artists: both Dall and Richards were at the head of their profession in the middle of the eighteenth century, and the scenes they shipped to the colonies must have been far superior to the work of the obscure William Williams who painted the wings and cloths at the earlier theater on Society Hill.

It is possible to piece together a fairly good picture of the stages in use in New York and Philadelphia just prior to the Revolution. Probably the Southwark and John Street playhouses were similarly equipped, and there is every reason to believe that their stages resembled those in use at the ordinary sort of English provincial playhouse of the mid-eighteenth century.

Royall Tyler's Jonathan, speaking of his trip to the John Street Theater, recorded the fact that "they lifted up a great green cloth, and let us look right into the next neighbour's house."[23] Thus the green curtain of earlier theaters was still in use at John Street. It is virtually certain, too, that the scenery Jonathan saw at the theater was shifted in the grooves common to English theaters of the period. We know, in any case, that this was the method in use at the playhouse later in the eighteenth century, for Dunlap recorded in his diary that "Warner, last friday fell from the Wing grooves above & received a serious hurt."[24]

In the English groove system the scenery was changed by the relatively simple process of sliding the various items of scenery on and off the stage as necessity required. The wings of the first scene, for example, slid off to right and left, revealing the wings for the scene that followed. In houses possessing sufficient overhead space the borders rose at the same time and were replaced by others that were lowered into position over the new wings. Conventionally, in better houses, a so-called back scene formed the rear wall of each new setting; as the wings and borders were shifted, the great back scene parted at center stage and the two halves were slid offstage in the same manner as the wings and replaced by new flats.

62

To guide and support the moving scenery, grooved timbers were used both above and below the pieces to be shifted. The lower grooves might be built into the stage floor or they might be constructed independently and pegged down at the required position; the upper grooves were suspended above the wings and back scenes rather in the manner of the upper track of a sliding door. In English houses of the later eighteenth century, the central portion of the upper grooves was hinged to swing up and offstage in two parts, like a pair of drawbridges, in order to lift the grooves out of sight when a tall back scene was used without masking borders. Whether hinged upper grooves of this sort existed at the Southwark and John Street is not known—indeed we have no real evidence that they were to be found at any eighteenth-century American playhouse, aside from the inherent likelihood of their presence. We do know, however, that they were used on American stages in the nineteenth century. In fact, hinged grooves very much like those found in eighteenth-century English playhouses still exist at a theater in Put-In-Bay, Ohio, completed in 1888 (Figs. 21, 22, 23).

The sets of grooves in use at the Philadelphia and New York theaters were undoubtedly placed parallel to the proscenium arch as they were in England. Such a practice seems to be a curiously unsatisfactory way of masking the stagehouse from patrons in the side boxes. But stage realism was essentially a nineteenth-century development, and it is unlikely that either British or American managers of the eighteenth century were in the slightest degree concerned that some members of the audience were afforded a peep into the wings during the performance of the play. The settings themselves, in fact, most often represented only a generalized background for the action of the play rather than a strict representation of a place filled with authentic detail. Although new scenery might·be constructed for the first performance of a new play, it would be used over and over again for any

63

21 / A set of upper grooves in the up position.
Town Hall Theater, Put-in-Bay, Ohio, 1888.

number of other plays with somewhat similar settings. Indeed, a good set of scenes might be employed at a theater until it had become so dirty and ragged and blackened by candle smoke that it was virtually impossible to tell what it represented.

Even had it been desired, a high degree of scenic realism was almost impossible to achieve on a raked stage that had been fitted out with movable stock scenery painted and constructed in artificial perspective. But the point is, of course, that a "slice of life" was not desired on the eighteenth-century stage; the more obviously "theatrical" a setting, the better it was appreciated by the audiences of the time. The very changing of the scenes in front of the spectators' eyes, for example, was considered almost as much a part of an evening at the theater as the play itself, and every scenic tour de force possible was incorporated in the plays and afterpieces performed in England and America.

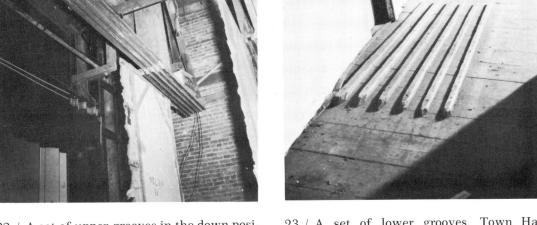

22 / A set of upper grooves in the down position. Town Hall Theater, Put-in-Bay, Ohio, 1888.

23 / A set of lower grooves. Town Hall Theater, Put-in-Bay, Ohio, 1888.

By the period of John Street and the Southwark, Douglass had acquired enough equipment to accommodate his audiences with a fair degree of spectacle. If he could not approach the scenic magnificence of settings like those created for the great London theaters, Douglass could at least approximate some of the less difficult trickwork employed at Covent Garden and Drury Lane. The so-called transparent scene, for example, had become a great favorite in the Douglass theaters by the late 1760's. In simplest terms a transparent scene was nothing more than a flat frame covered with linen or calico rather than heavier canvas and painted with dyes instead of the usual opaque scene paint. When lighted from the front, the wing or back scene appeared to be a conventional flat. When lights were brought up from behind, however, the scene faded or was supplemented by further painting on the back of the linen, and such effects as a sunset or a

65

burning building were made possible. Although the date at which transparencies were first used in the colonies is not known, it is likely that a scene Douglass advertised at Chapel Street in 1762 was a transparency of some sort. For a production of Lee's *Theodosius* the manager offered "a View of the Inside of the TEMPLE in its *original Splendour,* at the first institution of the Christian Religion at Constantinople: the Vision of *Constantine the Great,* a Bloody Cross in the Air, and these Words in Golden Characters, IN HOC SIGNO VINCES."[25] By 1773, and probably before, Douglass was beginning to offer transparent scenery at the Southwark and John Street. For a performance of *Cymon* at John Street, he announced "a Procession of the Knights of the different Orders of Chivalry, and the Shepherds of Arcadia, with a new set of Transparent Scenes."[26] Evidently these transparencies were considered something of an innovation, for on May 31, 1773, the New York *Mercury* recorded a glowing description of the novelty and beauty of the new scenic equipment.

By the middle of the eighteenth century the so-called back scenes found on English stages were no longer limited to a position near the rear of the stagehouse. At this time the sets of grooves that carried the side wings were frequently fitted out with additional slots for back scene flats, and settings of various depths became increasingly common. A scene might be played, for example, in a shallow setting, with those that followed taking place in increasingly deep sets until almost the full depth of the stagehouse was reached. It seems relatively certain that both the Southwark and John Street were equipped in just this way. In 1767 the first play written by an American to be performed by professional players was produced at Philadelphia's Southwark Theater. The play, Thomas Godfrey's *The Prince of Parthia,* contains a stage direction indicating that a divided back scene separating a shallow scene from a deeper one behind was necessary to the proper performance of the piece. In Act I, the first four scenes are set in the Parthian Temple of the Sun; at the beginning of the fifth scene the stage direction reads. "The Scene draws and discovers, in the inner Part of the Temple, a large Image of the Sun, with an Altar before it. Around Priests and Attendants."[27] There is no way of knowing absolutely whether Douglass produced *The Prince of Parthia* with the scene change as Godfrey wrote it. But the chances are excellent that the Southwark contained the necessary back scenes to accomplish the effect—and that the "Image of the Sun" was achieved by a transparent scene of some sort.

One other clue to the equipment in use at Douglass' theaters just prior to the Revolution perhaps deserves our attention. When the theater in John Street was constructed the dressing rooms occupied the space below the stage. Later, however, the dressing rooms were shifted to a new shed or ell attached to the theater.[28] There would have been no reason for an expensive alteration of this sort unless the area beneath the stage could better serve in some other way. Probably the additional space was required for new machinery. But the question of precisely what sort of machines were in use at John Street remains open. It may be imagined that, at the very least, the removal of the dressing rooms signified the introduction of one or more counterweighted traps, since the counterweight system and the supporting timbers would have taken up considerable space below the stage.

We have no idea what equipment was to be found in the files at the Southwark and John Street Theaters. Probably the relatively elaborate drum-and-shaft mechanism for simultaneous movement of borders and other scenic pieces was not to be found in these two relatively early playhouses. One imagines, however, that both houses possessed a crude gridiron from which drops were flown when needed in the action of the play, and the conventional sound effects apparatus, the rain machine and thunder run, which were located above the stages of English theaters. Both of these devices were of an engaging simplicity: the thunder run or thunder machine was nothing more than an ordinary

67

wooden trough arranged as a switchback. Cannon balls rolled down the first incline and thence into the lower run over some steps, presumably producing a roar that shook the whole theater. The rain machine was only slightly more sophisticated in design. A long, hollow shaft of wood was mounted at its balance point between two stationary uprights. A series of nails was driven into the shaft in a spiral pattern, with the ends projecting into the hollow center, and a quantity of shot was run from end to end inside the tube as it was rocked back and forth on its axis.

The methods by which lighting effects were achieved in England and America during the period just prior to the Revolution seem crude by modern standards. Yet even the rather basic equipment in use at playhouses like John Street and the Southwark must have been sufficient to light both players and scenery adequately. Above the forestage and within the stagehouse itself hung candle chandeliers, for the patent Argand burners were still a thing of the future. The footlights, however, were probably no longer mere candles with baffles to mask their glare from the audience, but a simple version of the oil floats used at British houses. In some of the better theaters of the British Isles these footlights could be raised and lowered by a system of counterweights, and perhaps such a scheme existed at New York and Philadelphia. It is more likely, however, that the footlights were fashioned from an ordinary metal box, rectangular in shape, that contained a number of pieces of cork pierced with wicks and floating in a bath of oil.[29] It is likely, too, that individual lamps— perhaps no more than saucers of oil with floating wicks—were placed behind the wings to aid in lighting the various parts of the setting.

Unfortunately we can deduce little more about the probable appearance of the Southwark and John Street. One fact is relatively clear, however: the Philadelphia and New York playhouses were the finest theaters to be erected in America prior to the

Revolution. There is no evidence that links either of the houses to an English prototype; yet both theaters were obviously conceived and constructed with English models in mind.

The finest American theaters of the colonial period were almost certainly modest indeed—but, in the half century since its beginnings, the American playhouse had achieved at least a reasonable measure of permanence and a degree of taste. From the construction of the John Street Theater to the prohibition of all theatrical activity just prior to the Revolution, a flurry of theater building took place in the smaller towns.[30] Little of value can be deduced from the information that survives concerning these buildings. It is almost certain, in any case, that none of them could compare with the theaters of Philadelphia and New York; but their very existence demonstrates clearly the continuing spread of theater building in the colonies. Perhaps, however, the Annapolis theater of 1771 deserves at least a brief glance, for the history of theater architecture in Annapolis from its beginnings to the years just prior to the Revolution reproduces in miniature the history of the playhouse in colonial America. We know that the first Annapolis theater of 1752 was little more than a warehouse converted to use as a theater building. By 1760 Douglass had constructed a new theater in the town that—although lacking any merit as architecture—was at least a proper playhouse. In 1771 a substantial little theater was constructed by the American Company at the head of West Street, next to Reynolds' Tavern, on land leased from the Episcopal Church;[31] it was a small, but neat and pleasant, country playhouse standing in a tasteful garden of flowers.[32] By the Revolution adequate playhouses had become relatively common, and the last twenty years of the century witnessed a great period in American theater architecture, a period in which the design of the American playhouse progressed far beyond the dreams of Lewis Hallam and David Douglass.

V / Town and Country Theaters after the Revolution

The Theatre at Louisburg is constructed upon as good a concerted plan, and has as cheerful an appearance as any erection for public exhibition as we ever remember to have seen on a similar scale.
(Charleston *Morning Post,* 1786)

On October 20, 1774, the first Continental Congress, in session at Philadelphia, passed a resolution aimed at prohibiting "all kinds of gaming, cock-fighting, exhibition of shews, plays and other expensive diversions and entertainments."[1] The pioneering age of American theater building was finished: Douglass' American Company disbanded and most of its members returned to Jamaica. Not until 1781 was another permanent playhouse to be erected on American soil. During the war, drama continued in the camps of the British troops and in the towns they occupied. In spite of the prohibition of the Continental Congress, drama continued, too, among the American forces. But, by and large, there was neither the time nor the money to erect new theater buildings. Temporary structures, or the permanent playhouses already in existence, were used by amateur players of both sides.

24 / Supposed view of the military theater (the log structure in the lower right corner), Charlottesville, Virginia, 1789.

Only one new theater was constructed in America during the war years. Late in 1779, a playhouse (Fig. 24), evidently nothing more than a crude log hut, was built by British officers interned at Charlottesville, Virginia. Thus, for some ten years, America was to witness the construction of only a single playhouse—and that structure was even less pretentious than the theaters built in the colonies more than half a century earlier.

Many of the theaters erected from the Revolution to the end of the century, in fact, were little better than those constructed in the era of Murray and Kean and Lewis Hallam. Most frequently these crude theaters appeared in areas that had not previously been able to support theatrical production: the more remote parts of the South, the western frontier, and the New England states.

In 1792 the first permanent playhouse in the city of Boston was opened to the public. The New Exhibition Room, as it was slyly labeled, may have been erected solely for theatrical purposes, although it is likely that it was nothing more than a row of wooden stables in Board Alley, later Hawley Street.[2] Christian Boston, as Samuel Sewall once feared, had finally gone beyond heathen Rome in the "practice of shameful vanities." But the first home of all the unspeakable horrors that Sewall had foreseen was surely a pitiful theater, and it was probably a relief to all concerned when, in June of the next year, it was announced that "the house will be taken down on the following Saturday."[3]

The same year that the New Exhibition Room was opened another building was converted to a theater even farther north, in the small town of Portsmouth, New Hampshire. A prologue read by Watts, the leading light of the company, described the undistinguished origin of his new playhouse:

> Then oh! the Conjurer favor with your nod;
> If you refuse, that self-same potent rod,
> Which from a warehouse reared this magic scene,
> Shall turn all to a paltry store again.[4]

Some two years later another crude theater was in use in the town of Portland, Maine. Converted from an assembly room, the playhouse seated less than a hundred spectators and possessed only a tiny stage, 15 feet wide and 7 feet deep.[5]

Thus, though relatively handsome theaters were already fairly common in the middle states, the companies in upper New England were operating much as David Douglass had some forty years before. Equally unimposing playhouses continued to be built in out of the-way corners of the South and in frontier settlements as far west as Pittsburgh and Detroit.[6] But even within the more important towns along the Atlantic seaboard, small, unimpressive theaters continued to be constructed, either as stop-gap measures until better houses were possible or as competition for the larger established playhouses.

The first theater at Richmond, Virginia, probably constructed sometime during the year 1784, was little more than a wooden warehouse or barn rather ironically located behind Rose's Brig, the Richmond city jail.[7] Hallam and John Henry's new theater on Philpott's Hill, constructed at Baltimore in 1786, seems to have been a building of equally small architectural merit, despite the claim of the managers that "the new Theatre is very commodiously built" and that they had "been at great expense in forwarding the completion of their plan."[8]

Two years before the end of the century, Nelly Custis witnessed a performance in Alexandria, Virginia, at a crude little theater that had been remodeled from another structure. She described the auditorium in a letter to a friend, Elizabeth Bordley:

[The theater] is a long work shop, very roughly done, wooden & small, there are four or five *benches,* one above another (like seats in an Assembly room) which are called the Boxes, then there is a kind of board partition made, and those seats beyond the partition, is the *Pit*—the *Gallery* is made by laying a few boards across the *rafters* of the house; on which the *Gods* and *Goddesses* mount at the hazard of their bones being fractured, in case of the boards giving way, there they make noise enough in all conscience; the stage is very near to the first row of boxes, one row of candles illuminates the whole, in the *Pit* the glimmering light, only serves to make darkness more visible . . .[9]

Yet the theater that so offended Nelly Custis was scarcely typical of playhouses in the more prosperous towns. Well before the end of the century, it is apparent that a merely adequate theater was no longer enough to satisfy the spectator in the larger towns; increasingly he came to expect comfort—and even a touch of luxury—as his due when he entered the auditorium for an evening at the playhouse. Before the return of the American Company from Jamaica in 1784, a new theater had been built in Baltimore by an English actor, Thomas Llewlyn Lechmore Wall, formerly a member of Douglass' company.[10] This playhouse, completed late in 1781, was obviously more than a jerry-built temporary theater, for it was constructed of brick and later sold for the fairly substantial sum of £2,000.[11] The Baltimore playhouse marked the beginning of a new era in American theatrical history. For more than a quarter of a century American theater had been a virtual monopoly of the Hallam-Douglass companies.[12] Wall's theater signaled the beginning of a period of expansion and increased competition between theater managers. The rising economic level of the country during the last twenty years of the century, the decline of hostility toward plays and players and, ultimately, the spur of competition led to more substantial playhouses.

In 1786 a theater of some architectural sophistication was built in the city of Charleston. The new playhouse, constructed just outside the city limits in order to avoid a £100 license fee, was built for a dancer and minor actor named James Verling Godwin who, like Thomas Wall, had begun his career with the Douglass company.[13] Everyone who described Godwin's Harmony Hall was impressed by the new building. A correspondent in the *Morning Post* wrote, before the opening of the playhouse, that he was "astonished to find such a beautiful little theatre could be constructed in so short a time."[14] Another writer, waxing equally enthusiastic, recorded his opinion that the building was "constructed upon as good a concerted plan, and has as cheerful an appearance as any erection for public exhibitions we ever remember to have seen on a similar scale."[15]

The playhouse that Manager Godwin erected at Charleston had cost no more than Douglass' Southwark Theater; yet, unlike the Southwark, it was no "ugly, ill-contrived affair." The sum of £500 that Godwin invested in his building could not have resulted in a very palatial theater, but at least the money had been used with a measure of taste not seen in the American colonies before the Revolution.[16] To a man the critics were enthusiastic; and even if one discounts much of the extravagant rhetoric of the day, it is clear that Harmony Hall was a better than ordinary playhouse. The overall arrangement differed little from that of Southwark and John Street: the conventional division into box, pit, and gallery had become firmly established in the better theaters by the early 1770's and was to continue well beyond the end of the century in many cities. But the Charleston house contained some refinements not known to have existed before the Revolution. Twenty-two boxes circled the pit, and about their use the *Columbian Herald* of July 11, 1786, reported: "Front Boxes are for parties of Ten and Side Boxes for parties of Six. Each Box has a key to be given to the Person who takes it."

The use of a key, of course, suggests a box door and, in turn, passages and a lobby behind the circle of boxes. Like the better British playhouses of the time, the new theater at Charleston must have possessed box passages at the sides of the auditorium and a box lobby or "crush room" at the front of the house. The number of spectators the various boxes held is also of some help in forming a picture of the auditorium. In British theaters of the day the front box area was often backed by a curved wall into which the crush room doors were let. Most frequently the front box area was somewhat deeper than the spaces given over to the side boxes. For the curved wall there is no evidence at Harmony

75

Hall; yet the fact that the front boxes seated ten spectators and the side boxes only six may mean that the typically English deep front boxes had arrived in this country.

If the benches in the boxes and elsewhere in the house followed English custom they provided only the barest minimum space for each spectator; as fine a theater as the great Covent Garden allowed only a grudging 21 inches "seat and void" to every patron, and on a crowded night the "void" presumably disappeared entirely.[17] If the benches at Harmony Hall were as crowded as one suspects, entrance to them from box passages or the crush room must have been difficult indeed. Often a bench securely fastened to the rear wall of each box, directly in front of the only entrance door, made access even more difficult. In at least one English theater, however, a portion of the bench in front of the box door was ingeniously hinged to swing upward each time a new spectator was admitted (Fig. 25).

The year 1786 saw the opening of another new theater in the South, Alexander Quesnay's Academy in Richmond, Virginia. Quesnay's Academy, in one sense, was not strictly a theater, for it was ostensibly built as a school. But Quesnay, a shrewd amateur, was not above earning a few extra dollars as a theatrical entrepreneur. Quesnay's Richmond building was actually his second venture as a theatrical landlord. In 1782 he had arrived in Philadelphia and opened the "Academy of Polite Science" after being refused the right to produce a French comedy and an English farce in the city.[18] It is evident that the Academy was nothing more than a device designed to skirt Philadelphia's theatrical prohibition. Continually harassed by the magistrates, Quesnay was eventually forced to raise the pit of his so-called academy to the level of the stage, dismantle the scenery, and turn his theater into a ballroom.[19] Four years later he met with substantially greater encouragement: the Richmond building, a large wooden structure, was a fairly elaborate and well equipped playhouse,

76

25 / Interior of a Georgian country playhouse. Note the hinged bench tops in the side boxes.

26 / The property room at Quesnay's Academy. Watercolor by Benjamin Henry Latrobe, 1798.

seating some 1,600 spectators and valued at approximately £3,000.[20] Little is known about the interior of Quesnay's Academy, but it is certain that the stagehouse was a large one and that it contained both adequate fly space and a trapped floor.[21] One feature of the building, however, is unusually well documented. On August 28, 1793, the managers, Thomas Wade West and John Bignall, inserted an advertisement in the *Virginia Gazette and General Advertiser* that mentioned some of the furnishings of the theater. The managers offered the public a reward of £20 for the capture of thieves who had broken open the playhouse and stolen, among other items, "upwards of 400 yards of printed canvass, one mahogony dressing table, six chairs, a pair of brass knockers from the stage doors, one pair of cast iron kitchen dogs, three sets of fire irons." Four years later, Benjamin Latrobe included a delightfully whimsical sketch of the property room at the Academy (Fig. 26) in his designs for a new theater at Richmond. Taken together, the description of the stolen articles and the drawing of the property room provide some interesting implications about the contents of a relatively good playhouse of the period. Latrobe's watercolor suggests, for example, that Messrs. West and Bignall had not lavished extraordinary amounts of money on the contents of their property room. But it must be remembered that a completely furnished box setting was not to appear on any stage for some years to come; a few tables and chairs and a number of hand properties were all that was really necessary on the eighteenth-century stage, and evidently this was the extent of the managers' collection.

Although Quesnay was French, it seems doubtful that his Academy was influenced to any great extent by Continental stagecraft or theater planning. It is likely, however, that the first New Orleans theater, erected in 1792, owed a significant debt to the French playhouses of the period. Le Spectacle de la Rue Saint-Pierre was built by two brothers, Jean-Marie and Louis-Alexandre

Henry, who had emigrated to New Orleans from Paris. The building, which stood at approximately the site of the present 732 St. Peter Street, was constructed by Jean-Marie, a self-employed carpenter and contractor, and was largely financed by his brother.[22] Le Spectacle, although small and of wooden construction, was a fairly substantial and well equipped building, for in 1794 the property, together with scenery and costumes, was valued at $8,000.[23] Little information about Le Spectacle de la Rue Saint-Pierre has survived: a supposed illustration of the building was reproduced in J. G. de Baroncelli's *Le Théâtre-Français, à la Nouvelle Orléans,* but it is virtually certain that the drawing is spurious.[24]

Continental theater architecture may have influenced the playhouses of at least one other eighteenth-century manager. In 1793, the French actor and manager Alexandre Placide leased the so-called Brick Market at Newport, Rhode Island, with the intention of opening a playhouse in the upper part of the building.[25] The old market house, which measures 35 feet by 65 feet, still exists and its exterior remains little changed since Placide's day (Fig. 27). Only a single trace of the Frenchman's theater exists in the interior. The auditorium that Placide arranged in the market house apparently remained undecorated until a short time before the opening performance. Then, dissatisfied with the appearance of his theater, the manager located an artist and set him to work on the auditorium. A fragment of one of the anonymous painter's murals may still be seen on the east wall of the second floor between two windows (Fig. 28). Sometime after the mural was painted, the walls of the room were thickened about six inches and the bit of painting that remains was left as a curiosity and covered with glass. The fragment measures approximately 36 inches by 57 inches and shows a small coastal or bay sailing scow, very crudely rendered in red and black. Probably similar decorations appeared in other parts of the room before the auditorium was destroyed and the walls plastered over.

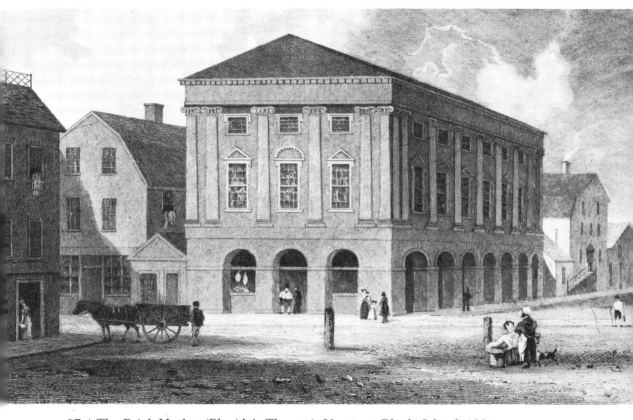

27 / The Brick Market (Placide's Theater), Newport, Rhode Island, 1831.

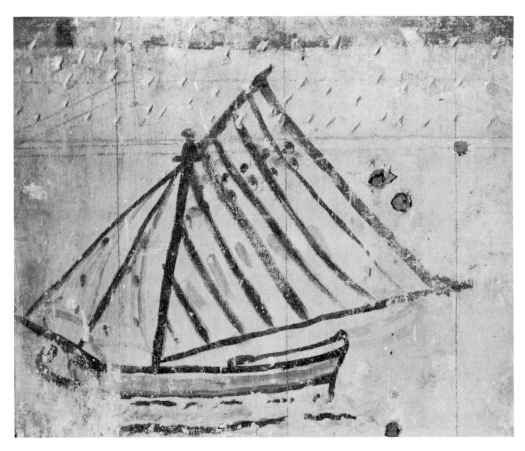

28 / Fragment of a mural from Placide's Theater, Newport, Rhode Island.

On April 12, 1794, Placide opened another playhouse in a brick building known as Solee's Hall on Church Street in the city of Charleston.[26] Placide's playhouse, known as the French Theater and later as the City or Church Street Theater, represented the manager's attempt to capture some of the business of the new Charleston Theater, erected by Thomas Wade West and his son-in-law and partner, John Bignall, in 1793.[27] West was the most prolific theater builder to arrive in America since David Douglass, and the story of the late eighteenth-century town theater is perhaps best told through his career.

VI / The Theaters of Thomas Wade West

Every attention will be paid to blend beauty with convenience, and to render it the first theatre on the continent. (On the proposed Charleston Theater, *New York Magazine,* September 1792)

In September 1792 the *New York Magazine* published a letter from Charleston, dated August 18, describing the proposed Charleston Theater:

On Tuesday last the ground was laid off for the new theatre on Savage's Green. The corner-stone of the foundation is to be laid the 20th instant. The dimensions are as follows:— 125 feet in length, the width 56 feet, the height 37 feet; with an handsome pediment, stone ornaments, a large flight of stone steps and a court yard palisaded. The front will be in Broad Street and the pit entrance in Middleton yard. The different offices will be calculated so as not to interfere with each other ... The theatre is to be built under the immediate direction of Mr. West. When it is considered that this gentleman has had 30 years experience in many of the first theatres of England; that he is to be assisted by artists of the first class, Captain Toomer and Mr. Hoban, we may expect a new theatre in a style of elegance and novelty. Every attention will be paid to blend beauty with convenience, and to render it the first theatre on the continent. The contractors have engaged to complete the building by the tenth of January next.

That Thomas Wade West had any great degree of experience in "many of the first theatres of England" is doubtful. One of the men mentioned in the August letter, however, was thoroughly experienced in his profession and had already gained some measure of fame; James Hoban, somewhat casually mentioned as West's assistant in the project, had created the designs for America's best known building, the White House.[1]

One is tempted to search for similarities between the drawing of the Charleston Theater reproduced in Eola Willis' *The Charleston Stage of the XVIII Century* (1924) and Hoban's prize-winning White House designs. But none exist, for the author was in error and the drawing she illustrates (Fig. 29) is not the Charleston Theater of 1793; it is, in fact, a crude sketch of Philadelphia's Arch Street Theater (Fig. 30), a building erected in 1829. Aside from this spurious drawing, there are no other reproductions or sketches of the theater, and its precise physical appearance remains a mystery; but contemporary accounts suggest the overall character of Hoban's building.

An anonymous correspondent in the *City Gazette and Daily Advertiser* wrote on October 18, 1794, that the theater was "executed in a style greatly superior to [playhouses] in any town of Great Britain five times the extent of Charleston." At the opening of the new playhouse on August 11, 1793, John Bignall, in the fashion of the times, spoke an occasional prologue that contained these lines:

> This night, altho' appall'd by hidden but soft rocks,
> We've launched a new-built vessel from the stocks;
> Fair, tight and clean—with care and cost she's made;
> A good and safe conveyance for our trade . . .[2]

85

29 / Spurious view of the Charleston Theater. Drawing by F. W. H.

30 / Arch Street Theater. Engraving by J. Yeager.

The quality of the verse may be doubtful, but the quality of the playhouse itself was undeniable. The letter from Charleston in the *New York Magazine* described the proposed interior of the building:

> [The stage] is to be 56 feet in length, the front circular, with three rows of patent lamps; the boxes will be constructed so that small parties may be accommodated with a single box; to every box there will be a window and a venetian blind; three tiers of boxes decorated with 32 columns; to each column a glass chandelier with five lights; the lower tier balustraded; the middle and upper boxes paneled; fancy paintings, the ground French white, the mouldings and projections silvered; in the ceiling there will be three ventilators. The frontispiece, balconies and stage doors will be similar to those of the opera-house, London.[3]

Almost certainly there were British origins for the new building; all of these features were common in good English houses of the day, and no American playhouse up to that time was anything like the Charleston Theater's equal. Since patent lamps were in use on the stage, it is possible that the glass chandeliers in the auditorium were fitted with the new Argand burners, although other theaters of the same period continued to burn candles throughout the house.[4] The decoration of the auditorium in white and silver is a significant departure from the older custom of painting the auditorium in various tones of green; from that time to the end of the century, no American playhouse is known to have been decorated primarily in the traditional English color.

For a year at least—until it was challenged by the elegant new playhouse at Philadelphia—the Charleston Theater was indeed "the first theatre on the continent." The building was warmly welcomed by the town. One correspondent summed up the feelings of the inhabitants when he wrote: "Whilst we express our approbation of the zeal and activity exerted by the managers, in the rapid erection and fitting up of this theatre—we must at the same time pay a just tribute of applause to the liberality and the taste evinced by them in the scenery, decorations and embellishments; which, however they may be exceeded by gaudy glitter, can nowhere be surpassed in neatness and simple elegance.[5]

However elegant and handsomely decorated, the Charleston Theater suffered from that common complaint of eighteenth-century auditoriums, poor visibility. One critic of the day wrote:

[The playhouse] is convenient within itself in every respect but one:—the two back seats of the upper side boxes require to be raised so much higher than their present situation, as the difference between a man's height when he stands and when he sits. Every person who has sat in those boxes in a full house must have felt the inconvenience of being obliged to stand up during the performance, unless accommodated with a front seat ... It is hoped that if the improvement recommended with respect to the seats of the theatre is adopted, the alteration will be complete; if they should be raised even higher than may be thought necessary to a convenient prospect of the stage, the spectators will be presented to each other in a more agreeable point of view.[6]

There is no record that the critical gentleman's improvement was ever adopted by Messrs. West and Bignall; however, another startling improvement was made in the house in 1794, and with it something approaching modern technology entered the American theater for the first time. On June 23 of that year the benefit of Mrs. Edgar was scheduled for the playhouse. The first advertisement carried a notice implying that the good woman's husband had created a new means of cooling the theater. It was probably no coincidence that Mr Edgar invented the machine just in time for his wife's performance; and one suspects that the curious device brought more spectators to the playhouse that night than did Mrs. Edgar in *"The Countess of Salisbury*, a celebrated Tragedy by Hall Hartson, Esq., presented here for the first time." The card published in the papers read:

> Mr. Edgar being informed that on the night of his benefit the audience were considerably inconvenienced with the heat, he has since that time been studying how to remedy the evil and is now most happy that he can announce to that public, whose liberality he so particularly experienced, that he has completed an air-pump of such construction as to render the theatre pleasant and comfortable, even in cases of crowded audiences. Mr. Edgar is indebted for his idea to the inventor of those air pumps that are often used on board ships of war . . . In public places in England, too, he has witnessed the utility of it, where its approved effect has been generally acknowledged . . . It is so contrived as not to intercept the view of the audience; it indeed takes up little room in the gallery, which then cannot hold as many as before, but the advantage which might arise from that, Mrs. Edgar cheerfully gives up for the general accommodation.[7]

It may be suggested that the air pump, as well as rendering the house pleasant and comfortable, probably rendered Mrs. Edgar totally inaudible. In any event, the fantastic machine seems never to have been used again at the playhouse in Charleston, although Mrs. Edgar remained.

In 1792 West had also begun work on another, smaller theater, in Norfolk, Virginia.[8] That the new playhouse, which was not completed until 1795, was not comparable to the relatively elegant Charleston Theater is shown by the manager's contract with one William Hobday in 1792, a document indicating that the new building was to cost £1,200.[9] Like most theaters, however, West's Norfolk playhouse proved to be more expensive than he had anticipated, and he was ultimately forced to borrow an additional £600 to complete the structure.[10] The building stood next to West's own Norfolk residence on the east side of Fenchurch Street between Main and Bermuda Streets.[11] The new theater, which was large and constructed of brick, was used as a playhouse until 1833.[12] As in Providence, the theater was later sold to a church, which occupied the building until its destruction by fire about 1846.[13]

It is not known whether the firm of West and Bignall used some sort of master plan for their American theaters. Certainly the Charleston playhouse of 1793 had not been arbitrarily designed from a set of stock plans or there could have been no need to employ Hoban. Although the Charleston Theater resembled English theaters and may have been roughly based on one of the provincial playhouses, it seems reasonable to believe that the final design was the creation of Hoban in consultation with Bignall and West. The Norfolk theater and the new Petersburg playhouse constructed in 1796 were, however, less elaborate buildings, and it is possible that these two relatively minor playhouses were constructed from a master plan.

The new theater at Petersburg, like the Norfolk playhouse, was a brick structure erected in a respectable part of town.[14] On March 30, 1796, West had received a deed from one John Grayson, merchant, to a site on the north side of Back (later Bank) Street, a little west of Fourth Street.[15] The theater West contracted for was to be 85 feet long, 45 feet wide, and 35 feet high, standing on a brick or stone foundation 7 feet high.[16] The total cost of the building and decorations was to be £1,000.[17] Begun sometime in April, the theater was finished in time to receive the crowds that came to Petersburg for the fall racing season in October.[18] The building continued to stand in the city until 1815 when it was destroyed in a fire that swept through Petersburg causing several million dollars damage.[19]

By creating a kind of composite of West's Norfolk and Petersburg playhouses and a theater erected in Providence in 1795, one can obtain a relatively good picture of the substantial town theater of the later eighteenth century. In 1794, a theater was remodeled from an earlier Providence building for Joseph Harper, formerly a member of Hallam and Henry's company.[20] Harper, who had previously played in the Providence courthouse, appropriated and remodeled an ell or wing of one Major McLane's coffee house. The Theater in the Old Coffee House, as it was called, was used for only a year and had been razed long before the coffee house itself was destroyed in 1855 to make room for the Bank of Commerce and an adjoining structure.[21] The building that replaced the Old Coffee House Theater in 1795 was a great improvement over the earlier theater; like its predecessor it was commissioned by Harper, but unlike it, the new Providence playhouse was erected specifically for theatrical purposes and was a fairly substantial structure.[22]

Harper's new playhouse was located on the corner of Westminster and Mathewson Streets. Fronting on Westminster Street, the theater was 50 feet wide and 81 feet long, with its principal facade pierced by three doors: the entrance to the boxes was in the center, the door to the pit on the east, and the gallery door on the west. Over the center door was a light wooden canopy, serving both as an ornament and as some protection from the weather.[23]

In 1814 the auditorium at the Providence theater was altered, and the result was a staggering tribute to America's prowess on the high seas. About the renovation George Willard later wrote:

Early in the summer of 1814, Mr. Warrall was sent here to decorate the theatre. Under his directions the embellishment was completed in season for the opening night. Over the proscenium was an Ionic entablature, the frieze adorned with a gold scroll ornament. On the centre, resting on a tablet, were the sterns of three ships, viz.: the *Independence,* supported by the *United States* on the right, and the *Constitution* on the left. The motto on this tablet was: "To hold the Mirror up to Nature." From this hung a crimson curtain with gold fringe and tassels. The ceiling of the proscenium was divided into panels of purple and gold. The dadoes around the upper tier of boxes was adorned with three tablets; those on the right and left contained representations of vessels which had signalized themselves; the *Wasp,* the *Hornet,* the *Enterprise,* and the *Peacock;* that in the centre contained the *Lawrence,* the *Niagra,* and the *Caledonia.* Rostrated columns contained the names of Hull, Decatur, Bainbridge Lawrence, Jones, Burrows, Washington, and Perry.[24]

From this description, and earlier accounts, a considerable amount is known about the Providence playhouse of 1795. It is clear that the house was fairly representative of the substantial town theaters constructed in many places after the Revolution. The exact cost of the building is not known, but it was virtually identical in every important respect with West's Petersburg theater, which cost £1,000. The dimensions of the Petersburg house were 45 feet by 85 feet; the Providence theater measured 50 feet by 81 feet. Both were equipped with two tiers of front and side boxes and a gallery. Thus, it is quite reasonable to believe that the Providence theater originally cost in the area of £1,000 to erect. As has already been suggested, this was no great sum, but it was quite enough to construct and furnish a first-rate small theater in the years following the Revolution; and the Providence theater was precisely that—a good but undistinguished play house.

The auditorium of the Providence house before its redecoration in 1814 was simple in overall character, but by no means merely adequate. Whether the interior of the playhouse originally contained painted decorations is not known, but by 1808 Mr. Warrall, the Boston scene painter who later added the elaborate nautical motif, was called to Providence to repaint and refurbish the house.[25] The employment of Warrall rather than a local decorator suggests that the redecoration of 1808 was no simple matter of laying one coat of paint over another. Indeed scene painters were commonly hired to design and execute the decorations of the better American houses as early as the eighties and nineties.[26]

The stage at the Providence theater was by no means large; presumably the actual stagehouse was some 50 feet wide and perhaps 20 feet deep, with the apron projecting into the auditorium for a distance of 10 or 12 feet. The actual proscenium arch is known to have been 24 feet wide and 16 feet high.[27] It seems safe to assume that stage boxes, and proscenium doors with their corresponding balconies, flanked the forestage at either side. The proscenium doors themselves must have been fitted with brass knockers similar to those stolen from Quesnay's Academy and seen in the print of Philadelphia's Chestnut Street Theater (see Fig. 37).[28] The old motto found at Drury Lane and at the earliest American playhouses seems no longer to have been used in the last two decades of the eighteenth century, and above the proscenium arch was to be found the phrase: "Pleasure the means, the end virtue."[29] Although it is impossible to prove, one suspects that the spikes that once formed a barrier across the front of the forestage and the box fronts had likewise disappeared as in later English houses, where only a decorative iron scroll remained to remind the spectator of the traditional metal spikes.[30]

31 / Stage curtain from the Providence theater. James Warrall, c. 1810.

Many of the better-equipped English theaters after the middle of the eighteenth century contained, in addition to the traditional green baize front curtain, a second "act curtain" or "act drop." The act drop was suspended directly behind the front curtain, but unlike it, was of canvas and decorated with a painted scene or other subject.[31] During its earliest years of operation the Providence theater possessed merely a simple baize curtain that marked not only the opening and closing of the performance, but the act divisions as well.[32] In the early years of the nineteenth century, however, a conventional act curtain was added to the Providence theater's equipment; this curtain, which still survives, may well be the earliest extant example of American scene painting (Fig. 31).[33]

Behind the proscenium arch at both the Providence and Norfolk theaters was at least one stage trap and perhaps more.[34] On April 16, 1801, the Norfolk *Herald* reported the somewhat unconventional employment of a stage trap in the Norfolk theater. The story is at once an important piece of evidence about eighteenth-century stage equipment and a classic theatrical anecdote:

> It is recommended to the manager to have a regular examination of the machinery below the stage; for on Tuesday evening, owing to the ponderosity of Mrs. Rowson, the springs of a trap door gave way, and not only the leading lady disappeared, but she carried little Mrs. Stuart down also. A sailor in the pit observed, that it put him in mind of the Royal George, which when she went down, sucked a sloop of war into the vortex with her, that was at anchor at a little distance.

What precisely the report meant by the "springs of the trap" is not known; probably he used the term merely to indicate that the trap door was raised and lowered by mechanical means. Conventionally stage traps of the eighteenth century were nothing more than simple elevators moved by a counterweight system below the stage floor; counterweighted traps in use on the modern stage, in fact, are constructed in much the same way as that which submerged the ponderous Mrs. Rowson.[35]

The trap doors mentioned in the account were probably the large, centrally located "grave traps" to be found on most stages of the later eighteenth-century English houses. It is possible, however, that some additional openings existed in the stage floor at theaters such as those in Providence and Norfolk, for there were a number of traps, cuts, and elevators in use on the English stage at this period. But there is no evidence for their appearance in the smaller American houses. This is not to suggest, however, that the more modest playhouses of the later eighteenth century were without the equipment necessary to create technical effects of some interest. By the eighties and nineties, for example, the transparent scenes that had so delighted colonial audiences at the best early houses had become more or less commonplace; simple transparent back flats were accepted as a matter of course and elaborate variations of this effect had begun to appear in the advertisements of theaters all along the eastern seaboard. In 1787 Charleston's Harmony Hall had included in its offerings: "A Splendid set of Portraits, large as life in Transparent Painting, Consisting of the following Worthies: Hancock, Adams, Ward, Hopkins, Ellery, Rutledge, Greene, Putnam, Gates, Wayne, Lincoln, Laurens, and Washington."[36]

At the Norfolk playhouse ten years later, the management displayed a most spectacular back scene for *The Maid of the Oaks* that represented "a double transparent arch, beautifully illuminated, in front of which is a triple arch adorned with various wreaths of flowers, grapes, etc., heightened by one hundred variegated illuminations."[37] It remained, however, for the old John Street Theater—still in use and presumably better equipped —to provide some of the most interesting work with transparencies and other devices. In the pantomime *Harlequin's Vagaries*, the managers reported, "will be introduced, a Series of Moving Transparencies, after the manner of Mr. Loutherberg's Ediphusicon. The whole will conclude with a display of Emblematical Transparent Scenery."[38] How these moving transparencies were created is not known, but it is altogether possible that an invention of Loutherbourg's was employed that cast fleeting effects on a landscape by the use of silk screens working on pivots in front of concentrated light from the wings.[39] In any case, Philip James de Loutherbourg and his famous scenic exhibition *Eidophusikon* were to have a significant influence on American stagecraft in the eighteenth century. Many of the pantomime entertainments produced at small American theaters were undoubtedly adapted from the spectacles of Loutherbourg. In 1797, for example, the little playhouse at Petersburg, Virginia, produced the pantomime of *Robinson Crusoe* as a portion of the scene designer's benefit. It was asserted that the scenery used in the production was especially designed by Robins, the scenic artist employed by the theater; but it is much more likely that Robins adapted Loutherbourg's famous scenery for the pantomime and reproduced the necessary technical effects only on a limited scale. Such a possibility is strongly suggested by the fact that, though *Robinson Crusoe* as it was originally designed by the Drury Lane artist contained eight complete changes of scene in the first act alone, the Petersburg production displayed only four scene changes in the entire pantomime.[40] If the smaller and less elaborately equipped theaters could not reproduce the effects seen at the London playhouses, they often contented themselves with selections from the great spectacles of the day. At Philadelphia's Southwark, for example, a curious hybrid of Garrick's *Stratford Jubilee* and the *Eidophusikon* was presented; and it was almost certainly a somewhat bizarre combination of the theater's stock scenery and specially constructed scenes and equipment:

> *Garrick's Ode* on dedicating a building to Shakespeare, with the original Music, Vocal and Instrumental; Scenery, Machinery and Decorations entirely new. The first painting will represent a Temple adorned with the statue of the *immortal bard,* Trophies, Foliages, and a new display of Moving Festoons. On the commencement of Shakespeare's Incantation, a dissolution of the building takes place and is succeeded by the two first Scenes from Loutherbourg's Eudiphusicon, representing a calm sea, the Moon rising, a storm, and Shipwreck.[41]

97

Several of the items mentioned at the *Jubilee cum Eidophusikon* provide evidence that the Southwark, like New York's John Street Theater, had been altered to some extent since its construction. The "new display of *Moving Festoons*" mentioned in the advertisement for the spectacle is difficult to interpret, but the logical explanation of the term would seem to be merely that ornamental borders raised and lowered by some variation of the counterweight system existed in the house by the last years of the eighteenth century. Probably these borders were operated by a drum-and-shaft mechanism. When a number of pieces were to be moved simultaneously, the drum-and-shaft system was an invaluable asset to the stage technician. If, for example, several borders were to be raised and lowered in unison their lines would be connected to pulleys at gridiron height and thence to a long shaft running the depth of the stage. On the drum of this shaft a line was wound in the opposite direction to the border lines with its free end attached to a winch. The turning of the winch revolved the drum and its shaft and simultaneously raised or lowered all of the borders.[42]

One additional item in the newspaper advertisement for the Southwark production suggests even more strongly that proper flies and a fairly complex flying system existed in the house by 1785. The Shakespearean temple was constructed so that "a dissolution of the building takes place and is succeeded by the first two scenes from Loutherbourg's Eudiphusicon." The effect mentioned seems to have been one of the most famous eighteenth-century stage tricks, the transformation scene. In simplest terms a transformation scene was one in which the rear wall of a setting disappeared or was altered in some way to reveal an entirely new scene. The trick was frequently achieved by the so-called rise-and-sink method. In this system the upper part of the back scene was detached from the lower and raised out of sight. The lower portion of the scene, at the same instant, sank into the cellar through sloats or cuts in the stage floor.

The newspaper advertisements of the last two decades of the eighteenth century illustrate clearly that an incredible variety of scenic apparatus was in use on apparently modest stages along the entire Atlantic coast. "The Fly," an arrangement of wire with a harness or perhaps a bosun's chair of some sort, enabled Mrs. West of the Norfolk playhouse to begin her ascent at the rear of the stage and "fly" to the topmost part of the upper boxes, returning "head foremost to the same place through a transparent sun."[43] At the same theater a balloon was made to descend on the stage during the course of a performance.[44] It might have been possible to employ one of the warm air balloons of the day to create the effect; it is much more likely, however, that a cloud chariot was used to simulate the descent. In any case there is sufficient evidence to believe that the cloud chariot was used at Alexander Quesnay's Richmond Academy in 1791, for a production of *The Tempest* as altered by Dryden ended with the "Spirit Ariel's appearing in A CHARIOT OF CLOUDS."[45]

The cloud chariot is one of the most intriguing of all scenic devices. In a real sense it was not an eighteenth-century device at all—the hanging basket of the *deus ex machina* is almost as old as European theater itself. But a version of the old basket of the Greek theater was a common feature of many English playhouses and, it would appear, of the later American theaters as well. The simplest form of chariot was little more than a wooden platform supported at each corner by vertical metal stirrups fastened in turn to lines that ran to the drum-and-shaft system above. At the rear of the moving platform was a profile piece representing clouds and extending somewhat higher than the head of an actor standing in the chariot, thus providing a decorative background and masking the backstage space. At the front of the chariot a similar profile piece covered the lower portion of the actor's body and, by the light of candles or oil lamps, gave him the appearance of being suspended in the midst of a bank of clouds.

The production of *The Tempest* at Quesnay's Academy is of

99

interest in another respect because it probably represents scenic design and stage machinery at their highest level in the less pretentious theaters. A fascinating pastiche of transparencies, transformation scenes, and other special effects, the production represented no small order of artistic and technical achievement if it lived up to the claims of the card inserted in the papers by Thomas Wade West:

> The opening discovers a troubled Herison and Tempestuous Sea, where the Usurper's Vessel is tossed a considerable time in sight, and gives a signal of an approaching storm, amidst repeated claps of Thunder, Lightning, Hail, Rain &c and being dashed on a Chain of Rocks, (which both sides of the stage strikingly represent) and at the same instant, a dreadful shower of fire, pouring from the distempered Elements, the crew gives signals of distress, the Waves and Winds rise to an affecting degree, and the vessel sinks in full view of the audience. The Scene altogether forming a most awful, but perfect picture of
>
> A SHIPWRECK.
>
> This hurrican (which is supposed to be raised by Magic) ceases a delightful prospect of the Enchanted Island appears, also of the Enchanter's Dwelling. Here the business of the play commences.[46]

Even after the "business of the play" began the audience was treated to the spectacle of Ariel in his cloud chariot and to such diversions as "a view of a calm sea, on which Neptune and Amphitrite appear in a Shell Chariot drawn by Sea Horses."[47] This sort of elaborate technical display would give a twentieth-century scene designer pause in spite of the modern equipment at his disposal; its production on the eighteenth-century stage must

100

have been both a marvel to the audience and a nightmare to the manager and everyone connected with the performance of the piece.

It is difficult to evaluate a production like that presented at Quesnay's Academy. By modern standards such an essay in spectacle as West's *Tempest* could scarcely seem more than hopelessly crude. Indeed, by the standard of the great London houses or even Chestnut Street and the Park, the Richmond production was probably only a few cuts above the amateur level. Yet, many of the scenic and mechanical faults that must have appeared in *The Tempest* as West produced it were undoubtedly overlooked; the creaking of the ropes that suspended the cloud chariot, or the sinking ship that was no more than a hastily painted profile piece were, in the broadest sense, conventional. That the ship was no ship and the chariot only a mass of wood and rope and canvas was perfectly understood, and the manipulation of scenic spectacle, when competently performed, was admired for its own sake.

This is not to suggest that the auditor of the late eighteenth century in even the more ordinary theaters would tolerate downright incompetence: what had passed for high art or simply been ignored before the Revolution was now considered an affront to the sensibilities of the audience. In 1787 a critic of the old John Street Theater wrote with some irritation about the shabby scenery at the New York playhouse:

Tho' we do not look for a theatre here conducted in so regular a manner as those in Europe, or the decorations so expensive and elegant, yet a proper respect to the audience, and decent and proper scenery, is and ought to be expected ... Surely the scenes should have as much the appearance of nature as possible; which those we generally behold at the theatre do not. For frequently where the author intended a handsome

101

street or a beautiful landscape, we only see a dirty piece of canvas; what else can we call a scene in which the colours are defaced and obliterated? Nor is it uncommon to see the back of the stage represent a street, while the side scenes represent a wood, as if two of the most opposite appearances must be put together to cause a natural effect.[48]

Not only poor quality on the stage, but carelessness behind the scenes had become offensive to audiences in theaters all over the country. Two years after the beginning of the new century the Norfolk *Herald*, which had previously catalogued the affair of Mrs. Rowson and the stage trap, burst into print once again with a critique of scene shifting and other matters behind the curtain:

> If the sound of the hammer, in the change of scenery, could either be avoided or lowered, it would be a great improvement; and although voices cannot be particularly ascertained, yet more discretion ought to be observed between the acts, behind the scenes. It is very grating, even at the most extreme part of the house, to hear vociferated, "d-mn your eyes," and "You blood of a b----." Private quarrels and jarrings ought not to offend the public ear; to those who sat in the stage box, it must have been distressing.[49]

But despite such occasional displays of choler in the public prints, there had been a great improvement in the stage and equipment of the American theater. Evident even in the smaller houses constructed after the Revolution, like those at Norfolk and Providence, and in additions to the facilities at such earlier theaters as John Street and the Southwark, the change was most dramatic at Federal Street, Chestnut Street, the Park, and in the designs of Benjamin Latrobe for the proposed playhouse at Richmond. From the construction of the Park Theater in 1798 to the end

102

of the century only a handful of theaters were built,[50] and only one of them, Thomas Wade West's Alexandria playhouse, was of any real architectural importance. It replaced a playhouse Nelly Custis described in March 1798 as a "long work shop, very roughly done, wooden and small,"[51] evidently a temporary theater in a place called Fulmore's Long Room, which had been fitted out for performances by an itinerant player named Christopher Charles McGrath as early as 1793.[52] Wade's theater, however, was already under construction when Nelly Custis wrote.[53] Plans for the playhouse had been mentioned in the newspapers as early as January 1797, and by 1799 the last significant American playhouse of the eighteenth century was completed on a lot on Cameron Street, opposite Gadsby's Tavern.[54] Built of brick, the new Liberty Hall, as it was called, was 50 feet wide and 90 feet long, and "inferior to few in the country for convenience, simple elegance and situation."[55] Like Placide's theater at Newport, the Alexandria building contained shops on the lower floor and a theater above.[56] Presumably the top floor of the three-story building designed by "Captain Stephenson, architect of Washington City" contained dressing rooms and storage facilities.[57] The designer had created a large building capable of holding some 800 spectators, and a durable one, for Liberty Hall served Alexandria until it was destroyed by fire in 1871.[58] It may well have been the last permanent eighteenth-century theater in existence when it was destroyed.

VII / Chestnut Street, Federal Street, and the Haymarket

The Stage is large and commodious—the lights numerous & good & the Scenery & Decorations may be justly said to partake of both the *beautiful* and *sublime*.
(Ezekiel Forman on the Chestnut Street Theater, 1794)

In 1794 the Chestnut Street Theater, one of America's best eighteenth-century playhouses, was opened at Philadelphia. As early as 1791 Messrs. Wignell and Reinagle, the managers, had expressed the desire to "unite in an undertaking for erecting a new theatre in some central part of the city."[1] Thomas Wignell, a cousin of Lewis Hallam and the son of a minor actor in Garrick's company and in various provincial houses, had come to America just before the prohibition of all dramatic activity in 1774. He and Alexander Reinagle, a musician, became partners after Wignell left Hallam and Henry's company because of a quarrel with the managers.[2] It appears that the partners had no trouble raising the money to finance their proposed playhouse, but found it difficult to secure a suitable lot.[3] Like many theater builders before and since, they were considered a serious threat to property values and a general nuisance by the more sober citizens of the community—the same citizens who owned most of the desirable sites for a theater. Some indication of the character of the forces allied against Wignell and Reinagle's venture is seen in a letter of October 2, 1791, from Ann Brodeau to Dr. William Thornton:

> I think I told you in my last of the opposition the Players have met with in their design to purchase a lot of Mr. Binghams & again of one in the neighborhood belonging to Palatiah Webster, but I hear they have succeeded at last & bought one of a Quaker preacher of your acquaintance, they got a third person to negotiate for the lot & he succeeded they were to pay £6,000 for it, it was no sooner known that it was for the players than Mr. John Dickinson of Wilmington (for that was the man) was pestered with remonstrances from all the persons in the neighborhood & they say he is yet struggling between interest and fame, the deedes not being absolutely signed when the remonstrance arrived, it is supposed that Avarice will triumph as it is not likely that any other person will give so great a price, the lot is joining his own house the corner of Chestnut & sixth Streets.[4]

It is plain that Mrs. Brodeau was a shrewd judge of character; avarice did indeed triumph, and Dickinson, a well-known lawyer and author of the celebrated *Farmer's Letters,* conveyed his property to Wignell and Reinagle.[5]

At the top of each of the stock certificates issued by the managers was a view of the contemplated playhouse (Fig. 32). It is possible that the theater shown on the stock certificates was designed by Wignell's brother-in-law, the London scene painter John Inigo Richards.[6] Charles Durang speaks of Richards as the designer of the building, although he also asserts, without citing an authority, that it "was a perfect model of the Bath Theatre, in England."[7] He was almost certainly wrong—at least in part—

105

32 / The proposed Chestnut Street Theater. From a stock certificate issued by the firm of Wignell and Reinagle.

for the facade of the Bath Theater (Fig. 33) in no way resembled the stock certificate illustration. It seems more likely that the designer of Philadelphia's new playhouse on Chestnut Street, whoever he was, borrowed heavily from the exterior of a theater designed for Limerick, Ireland, by James Lewis (Fig. 34). Both present a central Palladian motif of arches supported by minor columns and framed between larger pilasters, niches that contain statuary, wreathed emblematical devices, and a lower floor decorated in the popular rustic manner, which employed roughly hewn stonework as a contrast to smoother surfaces used elsewhere.

33 / Facade of the theater at Bath. Etching by T. Woodfall, 1804.

34 / Facade of the Limerick Theater. Drawing by James Lewis, 1788.

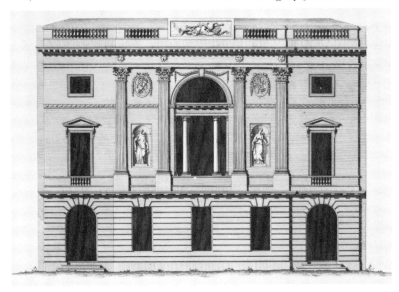

The building that was actually constructed, however, was a simplified version of the stock certificate view. Perhaps because of the high cost of the playhouse, $135,000—evidently a good deal more than the managers had planned[8]—the facade of the theater was drastically modified from the original scheme and, in fact, never completed until the early years of the nineteenth century. Although the building was ready for occupancy early in 1793, it was not officially opened until February 17, 1794.[9] A French traveler, Moreau de Saint-Méry, who attended an early performance was disappointed at the appearance of the exterior, pointing out that the playhouse "has nothing in its brick facade to suggest the public building. The entrance is mean and does not differ from that of an ordinary house."[10] An engraving of the theater made by William Birch in 1800 (Fig. 35) helps to make Saint-Méry's point clear. Although the central Palladian motif, pediment, and niches of the original design were retained, they existed only in the simplest form. For the elaborate rustication of the ground floor was substituted a rough wooden porch or shed, evidently used for shelter from the weather by spectators or the laborers already at work on the final stage of the facade.[11] Although the front of the building was not finally completed until 1805, another print by Birch, dated the previous year and perhaps based on plans for the new facade by Benjamin Latrobe, shows the building in its final form with a sixty-foot colonnade of Corinthian columns flanked by two fifteen-foot wings (Fig. 36). Some time before 1811, the two empty niches on either side of the Palladian window were filled with pine figures of Comedy and Tragedy made by the famous sculptor William Rush.[12] By 1811 the theater had assumed its final appearance, and, as James Mease suggested, was a relatively handsome building:

The Theatre in Chestnut, near Sixth street, was founded in the year 1791, and enlarged and improved, as it now stands, in 1805. It presents a handsome front on Chestnut Street of

108

35 / The Chestnut Street Theater (right). Engraving by William Birch, 1800.

ninety feet, including two wings of fifteen feet each. The centre building is ornamented with two spirited and well-executed figures of Tragedy and Comedy, on each side of the great Venetian window, over which, in two circular tablets are emblematical ensignia . . . The top of this centre building is ornamented with a pediment. The wings, opened by large windows, recede a little from the front above, but project below twelve feet, to the line of the street, and are faced with marble. These pavilions are decorated by emblematical figures, in tablets, and are connected together by a colonnade of ten fancy Corinthian columns. The extreme depth of the theatre is one hundred and thirty-four feet.[13]

36 / The Chestnut Street Theater. Aquatint by Gilbert Fox after the 1804 engraving by William Birch.

37 / Interior of the New (Chestnut Street) Theater, 1794.

Although Durang believed that Chestnut Street was modeled
on the Theater Royal, Orchard Street, Bath, the only surviving
view of the interior of Orchard Street, a watercolor by Nixon,
does not resemble the famous 1794 print of the stage and auditorium at the Philadelphia playhouse (Fig. 37).[14] This dissimi-
larity does not completely preclude the possibility that the interior
of the theater at Bath served as the model for Wignell and Reinagle's new playhouse, for the English building was altered

several times after Nixon's sketch was made and no illustrations of later states exist today;[15] but Durang's attribution is unsupported and remains dubious. The Chestnut Street auditorium's connection to the Limerick theater remains equally obscure. Lewis' designs for the interior of that building bear no special resemblance to the 1794 print of Chestnut Street and, in fact, contain cantilevered boxes, which definitely did not exist in the Philadelphia theater.[16] Thus, whatever the British origin of the building, conclusions about its stage and auditorium must be drawn from American sources.

Next to the famous Park Theater of New York, Philadelphia's Chestnut Street probably possessed the best-equipped stage and the finest scenery to be found in eighteenth-century America. The general character of the stage we know from the 1794 print of the interior of the house (Fig. 37). The print may or may not accurately represent the auditorium actually constructed at Philadelphia, but it clearly illustrates a stage and auditorium quite similar to those described by early patrons of the theater. The stage is known to have been some 71 feet in total depth and approximately 36 feet wide at the apron.[17] The 1794 engraving shows a flat front to the forestage and a curving partition separating the orchestra from the pit, although a plan of the building after its alteration by Benjamin Latrobe in 1805 indicates that the apron had been changed to include a semicircular front (Fig. 38).[18] In most respects the apron and proscenium arch were in no way extraordinary: conventional eight-panel doors with knockers flanked the arch and above them were the small balustraded balconies seen at most English houses of the period. In the less rugged era of the 1790's the spikes along the front of the apron had disappeared and all that remained at Chestnut Street was a long shield or baffle that masked the footlight trap from the eyes of the spectators. Perhaps the only unconventional item to be seen in front of the proscenium arch was the somewhat un-

112

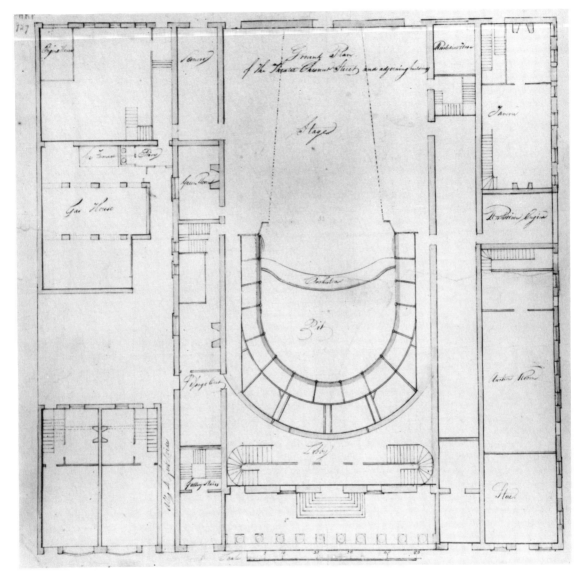

38 / Plan of the interior of the Chestnut Street Theater.

fortunate decoration above the stage, which featured the patriotic motto: "The eagle suffers little birds to sing."

Behind this earnest ornament, which contained a bank of clouds, an eagle, several figures and a giant serpent of doubtful configuration, may be seen a dark area that probably represents the lower edge of the front curtain. Behind this area in turn appear a number of perfectly flat undecorated borders. It seems curious that the borders are in no way matched to the foliage wings, but it is possible that the disparity was either the fault of the artist or, more than likely, merely the result of the typically casual attitude toward the combination of various pieces of stock scenery. The wings themselves represent rather ordinary foliage pieces cut in profile, and at the rear of the stage is an equally ordinary back scene or cloth. It may be that the dark lines at the base of each pair of wings are an attempt to represent the grooves in which the wings rested, but it is unlikely that the artist would have bothered to represent such pedestrian equipment. Grooves as well as even more elaborate equipment existed at the new Philadelphia playhouse, however, and it is certain that much of the scenery was of a relatively high artistic order. Critics were especially lavish in their praise of the new stage and the scenes that appeared there. One Ezekiel Forman wrote to a friend in 1794 that "the Stage is large and commodious—the lights numerous & good & the Scenery & Decorations may be justly said to partake of both the *beautiful* and *sublime*."[19] Another spectator wrote: "To judge from the dress and appearance of the company around me, and the actors and scenery, I should have thought I had still been in England . . . The scenery of the stage [is] excellent, particularly a view of the Skuylkill, about two miles from the city. The greatest part of the scenes, however, belonged once to Lord Barrymore's Theatre at Wargrave."[20]

The plot outline for a spectacular production of the pantomime

114   *Harlequin Doctor Faustus* illustrates the trickwork and scenic

effects that were possible on the stage at Chestnut Street within two years after its opening. It is impossible to know every scene or property that was included in the performance but it is certain that at least two transformation scenes of different types were included, as well as a scene that required the use of a cloud chariot, various trick properties, and at least eight separate settings:

Scene I. The Study of Faustus. II. Scene. Landscape and Water Mill. III. Scene. A cottage which changes to an Inn. IV. Scene. A street, in which is introduced a trick sedan chair. V. Scene. A chamber with a trick bottle and a Beauffet [Buffet], which changes into a book case. VI. Scene. Woods. VII. Cavern. The pantomime concludes with a view of the Temple of Glory. Aeriel spirits in the chariot and a grand Ballet.[21]

Several descriptions of the auditorium at Chestnut Street have survived. Of these, the comments of Moreau de Saint-Méry in 1794 are by far the most complete:

The interior is handsome. The arrangement of the boxes is in an agreeable semi-ellipse. The boxes are in three tiers, one above the other, fifteen boxes in each. Of these fifteen, each of the five facing the stage has seven rows of benches and will thus seat thirty-five people ... Each of the ten side boxes in each tier has two rows of benches and will seat four people in each row. Each row of boxes will seat 255, a total of 755 seats in the boxes. The pit is raked from the first tier of boxes to the orchestra pit. It contains thirteen rows each capable of seating about thirty persons, or a total of about 400.

The auditorium is painted gray with a gold design. The third row of boxes even has slender gilt railings of some elegance. The boxes, between which a small pilaster at the front almost blocks the view, are papered in tasteless red paper.

The auditorium is lighted by small four-branched chandeliers placed in every other box beginning with the middle of the second on each side, so that the upper rail of each tier of boxes has seven. Each hangs on an S-shaped gilded iron bracket. The orchestra pit holds 30 musicians in two rows facing each other. The forestage is large. The sides of the forestage represent the facades of handsome buildings but they face too much toward the stage so that they interfere with the view from the side boxes.

The acoustics are adequate. Vision is good from all points except from the rear of the second tier boxes where the slope of the floor of the third tier cuts off the top of the stage at the rear. And from other parts of the house one can see only with difficulty people seated in the rear of the boxes with seven rows of benches.

The corridors are large and commodious. In the upper part of the back wall of each box is a small shuttered window opening on the corridor to provide ventilation without the necessity for opening the door.[22]

Virtually everything described by Saint-Méry had already appeared in earlier American theaters, albeit in a less elaborate form. All of the features of the English auditorium that had been invading the American theater building since the earliest years of the century were present at Chestnut Street. The playhouse was, in fact, almost a complete summary of all that the American theater builder had learned from his English counterpart; it was nothing more than a first-rate English playhouse conceived and executed in the traditional manner. That it was equal to the great Patent theaters of London in its earliest days is doubtful, for the building was opened and operated for some years in an incomploto otato, without many of the conveniences common to the very best English playhouses. After its expansion and redecoration by Benjamin Latrobe in the early years of the nineteenth century, however, it is possible that the Philadelphia playhouse was equal in some respects to Covent Garden and Drury Lane, although on a smaller scale than either of these great English buildings.[23]

On April 3, 1820, the Philadelphia *American Daily Advertiser* reported the burning of the theater:

> The Citizens of Philadelphia have not, for many years, witnessed a Conflagration so awfully threatening in its appearance as was exhibited to them yesterday evening. The cry of Fire was first heard about a quarter after seven o'clock, and in less than half an hour, the whole of the New Theatre, extending from Chestnut-street to Carpenter street, was enveloped in flames; which, owing to its extensive roof, and to the scenery and other combustible matter within its walls, created an illumination over the city and for many miles round, more brilliant perhaps than was ever before occasioned by a Fire in Philadelphia. The heat was so intense that no exertions of the Fire-men could save the buildings adjoining the Theatre on the west—both the Work Shop and Gas House on Carpenter-street were destroyed, as were the upper stories of the two buildings on Chestnut street, and the Fire unsubdued, when this paper went to press . . .
>
> The roof of the Shakespeare buildings adjoining the Theatre on the east, was repeatedly on fire—but the incessant and active exertions of the Members of the Engines and Hose Companies eventually checked its progress on that side.
>
> There is reason to believe, that this melancholy event was occasioned, by some desperately wicked incendiary, and that the horrible deed must have been perpetrated several hours

before the fire was discovered, as it had gotten to such a head when the alarm was first given, that no human efforts could have saved the buildings which were destroyed.

All that could be recovered from the ruins were a few odds and ends from the green room and stage, and the two statues of Comedy and Tragedy.[24] The statues, which still exist, are all that remain of Philadelphia's finest eighteenth-century theatre.[25] Perhaps one other Philadelphia building of the nineties deserves at least a passing glance because of its unique interior arrangement. John Bill Ricketts, an English equestrian, constructed an amphitheater in the city in 1793, and a second and larger structure, in which both circus and stage performances took place, in 1795 (Fig. 39).[26] A later circus building, erected by Ricketts and John Durang in Canada, was modeled on the second Philadelphia house and suggests the way in which the characteristic theater interior of the period was adapted by circus managers. In his *Memoir* Durang wrote:

We where [were] compel'd to build the circus of stone all round, and put on a roof with sky lights, a coffee room. The circus was constructed in the inside the same as the Philadelphia circus: the box elivated, the pit in the front on the ground floor, our dressing rooms and satle [settle] where underneath of the box floor, a large stage orchestra over the door where the horses entered. I painted the inside myself. The doom was a light blue sky colour, cupids bearing garlands of roses round the circle, the boxes rose pink, pannels white, with a festooned blue curtain, the ring in panels intersperset with posts and gold chain leading round. The stage department was decorated with scenery, a curtain, a frontispiece, stagedoors, a niche on each with busts of armory.[27]

39 / John Bill Ricketts' Circus or Art Pantheon.

A surviving view of the interior of the Philadelphia circus, which burned in 1799, shows a good late eighteenth-century stage that has been cleverly adapted for a pony race by the addition of ramps leading to the pit area (Fig 40).[28]

40 / Pony Race at Ricketts' Circus or Art Pantheon, January 14, 1797. Etching by J. Galland.

41 / Obverse of a medal showing the facade of the Federal Street or Boston Theater, presented to Charles Bulfinch, c. 1794.

In the same year that the Chestnut Street Theater opened its doors, Boston raised a building that, in exterior design at least, was superior even to the Philadelphia playhouse. The Federal Street or Boston Theater, a house that John Bernard described as displaying "a taste and completeness that was worthy of London," was a brick building located on the northwest corner of Federal Street at Franklin Place (Fig. 41).[29] Designed by the famous architect Charles Bulfinch, it was a substantial and handsome theater that cost at least $40,000, and probably seated close to 1,000 spectators.[30] The building was 140 feet long, 61 feet wide, and 40 feet high, with a wing extending from the north side of the stage.[31]

Bulfinch, one of the first Americans to devote full time to the practice of architecture, was born in 1763, attended Harvard College, and after several years of study abroad settled in Boston to begin his practice in 1787. The Federal Street Theater of 1794 was scarcely Bulfinch's greatest work, although the arcaded porch with a simple colonnade above and the arched windows of the second story are related to the Boston State House, one of the architect's finest designs. As in typical English theaters of the period, the doors to the various parts of the house were widely separated, the principal door presumably leading to the boxes, that on the north to the pit, and the southern door to the galleries.[32] Curiously, this separation of the various parts of the theater caused the Puritan ghosts to rise again in Boston, and "opponents of the theater made strong use of this fact, alleging that by affording a special door to that portion of the house usually the resort of the vile of both sexes, a premium on vice was offered."[33] The rear of the building on Theater Alley was evidently similar to the front, with a series of arched pilasters ornamenting the central projecting gable.[34]

On the afternoon of February 2, 1798, a fire started in one of the dressing rooms of the theater.[35] Within a short time the fire broke through the front of the building and attacked the wooden columns and pilasters, and the original portico of the theater was either seriously damaged or totally destroyed. The walls apparently remained standing, however, and the building was re-opened on October 29 of the same year.[36] Charles Bulfinch was in charge of the renovation.[37] The damaged Corinthian portico was removed and an enclosed area erected over the open-arched loggia (Fig. 42). That the theater was not completely rebuilt is fairly certain, since both buildings look much alike and have identical measurements on early maps of Boston;[38] most probably it was only necessary to re-roof the original structure and restore the interior.

42 / Federal Street Theater after the remodeling that followed the fire of 1798.

The interior of Federal Street after the fire of 1798 is relatively well documented. Less is known about the theater as it was originally constructed, but a fairly adequate picture of its interior in 1794 can be gained from the information that has survived. William Clapp, in his early *Record of the Boston Stage,* gives a useful description of the interior of the house as it first appeared:

The stage opening was thirty-one feet wide, ornamented on each side by two columns, and between them a stage door and projecting iron balcony. Over the columns a cornice and a balustrade were carried across the opening; above was

123

painted a flow of crimson drapery and the arms of the Union and of the State of Massachusetts blended with emblems tragic and comic. A ribbon depending from the arms bore the motto, "All the world's a stage." At the end of the building a noble and elegant dancing room was constructed, fifty-eight feet long, thirty-six wide and twenty-six high, richly ornamented with Corinthian columns and pilasters. There were also spacious card and tea rooms, and kitchens with proper conveniences.[39]

The ballroom Clapp mentioned indicates something of the progress that the American playhouse had undergone since the early years. The ballroom alone was larger than the lot on which the second Williamsburg theater stood, and the chandeliers and free-standing girandoles in the room cost approximately one fourth of the total amount laid out by Hallam for the Williamsburg playhouse and lots.[40]

The molded decorations, columns, medallions, and pilasters in the house had been especially designed for the managers by a well-known firm of carvers and gilders, John and Simeon Skilling, apparently under the supervision of Bulfinch himself.[41] The exact appearance of the auditorium that Bulfinch originally designed for the theater is not clear, but the main facts about the house appeared in the building's contract. The auditorium was to hold 1,060 persons: 350 in 30 boxes arranged in two tiers; 280 in the pit; 280 in the gallery; and 150 in the slips.[42] The theater as it was originally constructed contained the main entrance on the front of the building, the loggia shown in early prints serving as a porte-cochere for the vehicles of the box patrons. The holders of box seats passed into a large lobby and up one of two stairways to the passages that lay behind the boxes; the less favored pit and gallery customers entered from the doors placed at the sides of the house.[43]

During the remodeling of 1798, Bulfinch introduced several important innovations into the auditorium at Federal Street. F. C. Brown suggests that the old front box area was rebuilt as a parquet, a subdivision of the house that was not to become common in England and America until the next century. The space in front of the parquet partition seems to have remained a fairly conventional eighteenth-century pit, flanked by passages and entered through doors near the forestage. After 1798, however, at least one tier of boxes surrounding the pit was cantilevered.[44] The use of a cantilever, of course, made it unnecessary to support the box fronts with columns that interfered with the spectators' view of the stage. Like the parquet, cantilever construction was uncommon in the eighteenth century. Richard Southern indicates, for example, that although cantilevered boxes appeared in James Lewis's plans for the theater at Limerick (see Fig. 46), they were not conventionally used in the London theaters until the 1860's.[45] The best architects working in America in the last years of the eighteenth century, however, applied the cantilever principle to auditorium design well before it became commonplace in Great Britain: cantilevered boxes appeared not only at the remodeled Federal Street, but at the Park Theater in New York, and in Benjamin Latrobe's plans for a playhouse in Richmond, Virginia (see Figs. 47 and 49).[46]

All three of these later theaters, together with Boston's Haymarket and the Chestnut Street Theater of Philadelphia, illustrate the increased size of the American playhouse in the final years of the eighteenth century. Prior to this time most American theaters had been modest in size, and even the greatest of the English playhouses were relatively small. By the eighties, however, the pattern was beginning to change on both sides of the Atlantic. Quesnay's Academy, constructed in 1786 at Richmond, Virginia, was a comparatively large house with room for 1,600 spectators, and the rebuilt Drury Lane of 1794 seated 3,611 as

125

against some 2,000 in previous years.[47] This taste for larger houses, together with the introduction of more complex stage machinery, resulted in the employment of an increasingly large number of stage hands and other functionaries. At Federal Street, for example, a Mr. Stevens and his wife were both employed to tend the stage door, and behind the scenes a full-time chief mechanic, wardrobe keepers, lamp keepers, fire keepers, dressers, and a call boy all pursued their vital occupations.[48]

A small part of the equipment owned by the Federal Street Theater was recorded in an inventory of "Additional Scenery," and even the few items mentioned suggest strongly the increasing complexity of stage machinery in the large houses, and the necessity of a trained mechanic to superintend the production of elaborate visual and sound effects. The list contains a fascinating variety of scenes and machines, some of which demonstrate clearly the potential of the stage at the new playhouse in Federal Street: "A Sun rise Scene, distant Tower, arches & Machinery & crimson transparent Shades, Large Ship to Sink, rock Wings & Machinery—Wind Machine, Iron Windlace &c.: New Rocks & Cave Entrance, Steps, Scaffold, planks & tressells."[49] The transparent scenery, of course, was not uncommon; but the reference to a "Large Ship to Sink" suggests that more unusual stage equipment existed at the theater. Probably the ship mentioned was little more than a large cut-out flat that descended through one of the narrow openings in the stage floor, although possibly it was a three-dimensional model like that used on the stage of the Park Theater in 1799, which was "not as is usual on such occasions, a mere profile, but a perfect model."[50] A three-dimensional piece of this sort would, however, have required the use of elaborate trap or "bridge" equipment to raise and lower the ship, and it is not known that Federal Street possessed such a luxury as a movable bridge. It is quite likely, however, that the

126

theater was equipped with the vision steps seen in better British playhouses of the period. The steps mentioned in the account of additional scenery at the theater may, of course, have been merely a common run of stairs; but a trained stage mechanic could have constructed vision steps with little difficulty, and it may be imagined that so well-equipped a house as Federal Street possessed such a device. As the name implies, vision steps were an apparatus designed to produce a vision or ghost effect during the course of a performance. Commonly, the steps used in such an effect were hinged to the front of the carpenter's gallery at the rear of the stage and swung upward and back when not in use. When the vision effect was required the steps were lowered by means of ropes and pulleys and the actor impersonating the ghost or spirit descended them from the carpenter's gallery at the same time that the upper back shutters were drawn away: thus the "ghost walked" high above the heads of the other actors and in the comparative darkness at the rear of the stagehouse. With only a lighted candle in his hand, the actor would undoubtedly have seemed to float in mid-air, and the effect must surely have been one of the most interesting on the stages of the eighteenth century.

Perhaps the most important description of late eighteenth-century stage equipment, however, comes not from the Federal Street Theater but from Boston's other playhouse, the Haymarket. In 1796 Charles Stuart Powell, the former manager of Federal Street, erected near the corner of Tremont and Boylston Streets a new building known as the Haymarket Theater. The new Boston playhouse was capitalized at $12,000, less than the amount originally allotted for Federal Street.[51] Although the Haymarket was substantially larger than Federal Street, Powell's second theater was hardly the peer of his first in taste or architectural sophistication. A watercolor painting of the theater

(Fig. 43) indicates that William Dunlap's description of the Haymarket as "an immense building, entirely constructed of wood" is painfully accurate.[52] There is little more to say: Powell's new playhouse was obviously built to accommodate a large number of spectators and all other considerations seem to have been somewhat incidental. It's name at once suggests some connection with the similarly named London theaters. As the early watercolor indicates, however, the playhouse was named for its proximity to an actual Boston haymarket; it is mere coincidence that it bore the same name as two of England's most famous theaters.

Little is known about the interior appearance of the Haymarket. Probably, however, it possessed an auditorium of no great taste or style. John Bernard, in any case, speaks rather slightingly of the Haymarket in comparison to Federal Street, and Dunlap avoids the whole issue by indicating merely that "it had three tiers of boxes and a gallery. The lobbies and staircases were spacious and convenient ... The entrance to the pit was up a flight of steps."[53] The Haymarket was a further example of the increasing size of the American playhouse in the last decade of the eighteenth century, but it was scarcely one of America's greatest theaters.

From the Haymarket Theater comes the only significant, extensive account of eighteenth-century American stagecraft. On February 20, 1797, an American play by John D. Burk, *Bunker Hill, or the Death of General Warren,* was first performed at the playhouse. Some time later, Burk wrote to John Hodgkinson about the play and, in his letter, provided a detailed account of the means by which the scenery was constructed and the effects achieved:

The hill is raised gradually by boards extended from the stage to a bench. Three men should walk abreast of it, and the

43 / The Haymarket Theater (center, rear). Watercolor by Robertson, 1798.

side where the English march up, should for the most part be turned towards the wings; on our hill there was room for eighteen or twenty men, and they were concealed by a board painted mud colour, and having two cannons painted on it—which board was three feet and a half high. The English marched in two divisions from one extremity of the stage, where they ranged, after coming from the wings, when they come to the foot of the hill. The Americans fire—the English fire—six or seven of your men should be taught to fall—the fire should be frequent for some minutes. The English retire to the front of the stage—second line of English advance from the wing near the hill—firing commences—they are again beaten back—windows on the stage should be opened to let out the smoak. All the English make the attack and mount the hill. After a brisk fire, the Americans leave works and meet them. Here is room for effect, if the scuffle be nicely managed. Sometimes the English falling back, sometimes the Americans—two or three Englishmen rolling down the hill. A square piece about nine feet high and five feet wide, having some houses and a meeting-house painted on fire, with flame and smoak issuing from it, should be raised two feet distance from the horizon scene at the back of your stage, the windows and doors cut out for transparencies—in a word it should have the appearance of a town on fire. We had painted smoak suspended—it is raised at each wing, and is intended to represent Charleston, and is on a line with the hill, and where it is lowest. The fire should be played skillfully (this puts one in mind of Bottom playing moonshine) behind this burning town, and the smoak to evaporate. When the curtain rises in the fifth, the appearance of the whole is good —Charleston on fire, the breastwork of wood, the Americans appearing over the works and the muzzles of their guns, the English and the American music, the attack of the hill, the falling of the English troops, Warren's half descending the hill and animating the Americans, the smoak and confusion, all together produce an effect scarce credible. We had a scene of State Street—if you had one it would not be amiss—we used it instead of the scene of Boston Neck—it appears to me you need not be particular, but the hill and Charleston on fire ... Small cannon should be fired during the battle, which continued with us for twelve or fifteen minutes. I am thus prolix that you may find the less difficulty in getting it up—it is not expensive, and will always be a valuable stock piece ... We had our hill on the left side of the stage—the painting of Charleston on fire should not be seen till the fifth act.[54]

It is interesting to note that the frontispiece to an earlier play on the same theme, Hugh Henry Brackenridge's *The Battle of Bunker's Hill* (1776), shows the climactic scene of Warren's death on the hill with a back cloth very similar to that which Burk described. It is very likely, in fact, that the rather basic setting described by Burk was taken from the illustration that accompanied the printed version of the earlier work.[55] In any case, the description of the scenery for Burk's play, though valuable as an account of eighteenth-century technical practice, illustrates very little sophisticated use of materials on the stage at Boston's Haymarket. It remained for New York's Park Theater to set truly high standards of scene design and technology for the American playhouse of the eighteenth century.

VIII / The Park and the Proposed Richmond Theater

But don't you think, after all, there is rather a—sort of a—kind of a *heavyishness* about the house? don't you think it has a little of an *undergroundish* appearance?
(Washington Irving on the Park Theater)

In 1798 the city of New York received a new theater that compared favorably with the finest playhouses of Philadelphia and Boston. The Park Theater (or New Theater as it was first called) was opened on January 29, 1798.[1] As was so often the case in the eighteenth century, expenses had spiraled at a tremendous rate, and the managers, William Dunlap and John Hodgkinson, were forced to open the playhouse before it was completely finished. The cost of the building, which they had hoped to erect for slightly more than $42,000, rose to over $130,000.[2] That sum is very close to the amount that Wignell and Reinagle—much against their will—had lavished on the Philadelphia theater constructed several years before, and more than three times the amount spent by Powell on his handsome theater in Federal Street.

The Park Theater was undeniably a splendid building. A view of the theater is extant (Fig. 44) and, although it represents the proposed playhouse rather than the theater that was actually constructed, it is reasonably close to the descriptions of the Park that have survived.[3] Joseph Ireland, for example, states that the building actually erected in Park Row was "three stories high, of stone, with about six steps up to the box entrance."[4] Although hardly in the nature of conclusive proof, Ireland's description is obviously of a building similar to that shown in the early print. Another writer is more helpful:

[The engraving] is literally correct, except in the introduction of the United States coat-of-arms on the facade, for this national emblem, though in the original design, was never completed. The rude extension on the left was used for rehearsals, and was so loosely constructed that the "boys of the period" used to assemble in the open lot in front to catch glimpses of the mimic scenes within. Three of the fine porticoes opened to the vestibule, from which there were three doors—the centre one leading into the "ticket office" and "managers" room.[5]

Various other reports about the building verify this description of the wing and the arcade. Presumably, then, the theater as it was ultimately constructed did not differ widely from the original designs, though it is certain that a statue of Shakespeare was substituted for the rampant eagle on the tympanum, apparently in a niche let into the pediment.

There is some confusion about the responsibility for the Park's overall design. It has been stated that the building was the work of the French architect and engineer Marc Isambard Brunel, and that Brunel in turn had adapted his building from some other unknown source.[6] A newspaper account of the period, however,

133

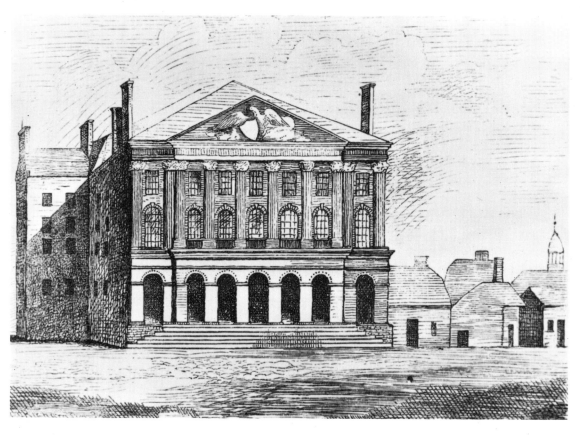

44 / New Theater (Park Theater) in New York. Engraving by Tisdale.

speaks of "Messrs. Mangino [oio], who were the architects of the house ..."[7] Brunel was evidently a clerk in the office of the Mangin brothers at this time, but the Park was probably the work of Joseph Mangin, the designer of the New York City Hall.[8]

The Park was a large theater for its time and place. According to Ireland, it was some 80 feet wide and 165 feet long, measurements that are logical enough in view of the theater's seating capacity of about 2,000.[9] If these figures are correct, the Park was the largest theater (at least in terms of audience capacity) built in America before the turn of the eighteenth century.

It is definitely known that the Park, like Federal Street, originally contained cantilevered boxes. The fact is reported in a newspaper account of the day,[10] and is discussed in some detail by William Dunlap: "As the Park theatre was originally constructed, and as it remained until the proscenium was remodeled by Mr. Holland, there were no pillars as props to the upper boxes: they were supported by timbers projecting from the walls, and appeared, with their tenons, self-balanced.[11] The similarity of the Park's facade to the proposed Chestnut Street exterior, and the use of cantilevered boxes like those of the Limerick theater, suggest some influence from both buildings rather strongly, but there is no real proof that they served as models for other details.[12]

Little is known about the original appearance of the auditorium at the Park, for it was altered to some extent in 1798, 1799, and 1802, and completely gutted and rebuilt in 1807.[13] No eighteenth-century print of the interior in any of its states is known to exist.[14] Two newspaper accounts, however, are of some help in reconstructing the auditorium as it appeared at the opening of the theater in 1798. A correspondent in the *Commercial Advertiser* of January 31 reported:

The audience part of the New Theater is a segment of a large circle—and of course the spectators, even in the front boxes,

135

are brot within a very convenient distance, both for seeing and hearing. The Pit is remarkably commodious. The Boxes are disposed in three semi-circular rows, from one side to the other of the stage—and the Gallery is thrown back of the upper front boxes. The total omission of pillars as supports to the boxes, avoids a common and great obstacle (in Theaters) to the view—and when the house is filled, presents an unbroken line of spectators, which forms no uninteresting part of the *spectacle.*

The *Daily Advertiser* of the same date expressed somewhat similar thoughts about the newly opened house:

> The essential requisites of hearing and seeing have been happily attained. We do not remember to have been to any Theatre where the view of the stage is so complete from all parts of the house, or where the actors are heard with such distinctness.
>
> The house is made to contain about 2,000 persons. The audience part, though wanting in those brilliant decorations which the artists have designed for it, yet exhibited a neatness and simplicity which were highly agreeable.

A year later "the decorations which the artists have designed" were seemingly put in place. By the first years of the new century, however, the interior of the Park may well have lost much of its glitter—or so it seemed to Washington Irving, the famous "Jonathan Oldstyle" of the *Morning Chronicle.* Irving visited the Park often and was unimpressed by the house. One sample of his criticism makes his objections clear:

> And what, pray, is the use of that chandelier, as you call it, that is hung up among the clouds, and has showered down its favours upon my coat?

Oh, that is to illumine the heavens, and set off to advantage the little perriwig'd cupids, tumbling head over heels, with which the painter has decorated the *dome*. You see we have no need of the chandelier below, as here the house is perfectly well illuminated; but I think it would have been a great saving of candle-light, if the manager had ordered the painter, among his other pretty designs, to paint a moon up there, or if he was to hang up that sun with whose *intense light* our eyes were annoyed in the beginning of the afterpiece.

But don't you think, after all, there is rather a—sort of a—kind of a *heavyishness* about the house? don't you think it has a little of an *undergroundish* appearance?[15]

Oldstyle's criticisms aside, the interior of the Park was the best that America had to offer in the eighteenth century; if any American playhouse of the period approached the splendor of England's Patent houses, it was almost certainly the great new theater erected in New York. In a sense, however, it is not possible to speak of the Park as a truly representative eighteenth-century theater. The evidence suggests that it was America's first transitional playhouse, combining in its auditorium typical eighteenth-century features and certain innovations more characteristic of later houses. In the second tier of seats facing the stage was an area commonly known as the Shakespeare box that seated some 200 or 300 spectators and probably covered almost the entire end of the auditorium.[16] The Shakespeare box was a box in name only, for so large a space can only properly be termed a gallery; and above it was yet another gallery, of a tremendous size, which probably extended back over the lobby space behind the auditorium.[17] Thus, the Park, in its earliest days, contained the traditional front and side boxes only on the lowest level: the second level contained side boxes and a gallery; and the uppermost level, side boxes and a deeper gallery still. A similar arrangement was

137

to be found in some of the best English theaters of the period, for the conventional Georgian scheme of box, pit, and gallery was slowly disappearing as a new type of auditorium evolved.[18] The Park, no less than the theaters of England, illustrated this movement away from the playhouse of Cibber and Pepys—and toward the theater of the Victorian period.

The stage at the Park was almost certainly the best equipped in an American playhouse before the turn of the eighteenth century, and it contained spectacles of a lavishness never seen before by an American audience. Most of the information about the stage and equipment in use at the Park must be drawn from accounts of the productions at the theater, but at least a small amount of descriptive material concerning the stage has survived. At either side of the stage were *faux marble* columns and the usual proscenium doors fitted with large lion-headed knockers and topped by latticed proscenium windows or balconies. Over the proscenium arch was painted a gorgon head and a copy of the motto, in Greek, which had appeared at the temple of Delphi, "Know Thyself."[19] The main curtain was no longer merely a poor object of green baize but was constructed of blue mohair fringed with gold and contained, in the center, a golden lyre with the inscription, "To hold the Mirror up to Nature."[20] Washington Irving, as was his wont, managed to find the proscenium arch and the curtain more than a little pompous and foolish. In the character of Jonathan Oldstyle he wrote:

By the by, my honest friend was much puzzled about the curtain itself. He wanted to know why that *carpet* was hung up in the theatre? I assured him it was no carpet, but a very fine curtain. And what, pray, may be the meaning of that gold head, with the nose cut off, that I see in front of it? The meaning—why, really, I can't tell exactly—though my cousin, Jack Stylish, says there is a great deal of meaning in it. But surely you like the *design* of the curtain? The design,—why really I can see no design about it, unless it is to be brought down about our ears by the weight of those gold heads, and that heavy *cornice* with which it is garnished. I began now to be uneasy for the credit of our curtain, and was afraid he would perceive the mistake of the painter, in putting a *harp* in the middle of the curtain, and calling it a *mirror;* but his attention was *happily* called away by the *candle-grease* from the chandelier, over the centre of the pit, dropping on his clothes.[21]

Other critics of the theater, however, were substantially less waspish than Oldstyle. In accounts of the building's interior the stage and scenery at the new theater were accorded the highest praise. The *Daily Advertiser* of January 31, 1798, remarked: "The stage was everything that could be wished. The scenery was executed in a most masterly style. The extensiveness of the scale upon which the scenes are executed, the correctness of the designs, and the elegance of the painting, presented the most beautiful views which the imagination can conceive. The scenery was of itself worth a visit to the theatre." The *Commercial Advertiser* of the same date reported, in even more glowing terms: "The stage is remarkably commodious—and no language will give the reader an adequate idea of the scenery, which is universally spoken of as surpassing for elegance and effect, everything of the kind heretofore seen in America."

The phrase employed by the *Commercial Advertiser* was well chosen, for it is apparent that the scenery did indeed surpass "everything of the kind heretofore seen in America." All of the scenic effects seen on earlier stages were present at the Park, and far more splendidly managed than had previously been possible at any other American playhouse. The variety and the technical skill apparent in the scenery at the new theater is considered at length by George C. D. Odell in his *Annals of the New York Stage,* and there is little point in attempting to summarize his work on the subject.[22] But a few examples of the kind of settings in use at the Park will help to establish the tremendous artistic and technical scope of the scenic department and the great variety of scenes and machines that must have been used on the stage. Selected plays from the months of May and June 1799 provide a good picture of the Park's offerings in the final year of the eighteenth century and the first season of the theater's operation. On May 13, New York audiences were treated to Shakespeare's *Henry VIII:*

> In act 1st, the grand Banquet of Cardinal Wolsey.
> In act 2d, the Procession of the Duke of Buckingham to execution.
> In act 3d, the Trial of Queen Catherine.
> In act 4th, the grand Coronation of Anna Bullen, with the mode and manner of delivering the usual challenge Given by the Champion of England, on Horseback.
> In act 5th, the Christening of the Princess Elizabeth.[23]

If there be any doubt that live horses were used in the May production of *Henry VIII,* it is speedily removed by a glance at the fantastic spectacle arranged for Thomas Abthorpe Cooper's benefit on June 3. During the course of the evening's performance of *Coriolanus* were exhibited:

> In act 2d, a Grand TRIUMPHAL ENTRY.
> *The order of the procession as follows:*
> Two Boys bearing Incense,
> An Officer with a Roman Eagle,
> Eight Senators, Four Trumpets,

140

Two Boys bearing Incense,
Four Priests with Torches,
Two Officers,
Six Lictors with Fasces,
Two Officers with Standards,
Six Soldiers bearing a Bier laden with Spoils.

A CHOIR consisting of

Four Boys,	Six Virgins,
Four Priests with Torches,	Six Lictors with Fasces.

Senators—Soldiers—Standard Bearers—Fifes—Drums—
Trumpets—Priests, &c. &c.

A CAPTIVE GENERAL IN CHAINS

Volumnia, Virgilia, Valeria

Six Virgins strewing Flowers, before a Triumphal Car,
bearing CORIOLANUS, drawn by

TWO WHITE HORSES,

Accompanied with a full band of Instrumental Music, and
a Grand Chorus,

"See the Conquering Hero comes"

Such an elaborate pageant, with its accompanying scenery
and livestock, must have required the use of almost the full
depth of the stage at the Park, and the spectacle that followed
two days later surely tested the mettle of both the scene painters
and the mechanics employed at the new house. This offering was
The Constellation, or *American Triumph*, and the public was
informed:

In the course of the Entertainment will be accurately exhibited, the various circumstances which took place on this
Glorious Occasion.

The Constellation in Chase of l'Insurgente, and making Sig-
nals; which not being properly answered, the Constellation
crowds a great press of Sail, when l'Insurgente display [*sic*]
the French Flag, and fires a gun to windward. Shortly after,
her main-top-mast goes by the cap, and the action commences with a broadside from the Constellation. In the
course of the action, l'Insurgente is raked fore-and-aft three
times; and finally striking, she is boarded, and the American
flag triumphantly displayed. The representation of the Constellation is not as is usual on such occasions, a mere profile,
but a perfect model.

Such were the displays of spectacle seen on the stage of the
Park Theater in the final year of the eighteenth century; in the
years that followed they were to become both increasingly elaborate and increasingly realistic. In the early nineteenth century
greater pains were taken with the details of the settings, and it
is even possible, as Odell speculates, that a simple form of the
box set was in use on the stage at the Park well before it had become a convention of scene design.[24] The Park, constructed with
proscenium doors in the typical eighteenth-century fashion,
possessed a stage that was antithetical to the realistic setting.
But, as we shall see, the last great American theater of the century, Benjamin Latrobe's proposed Richmond playhouse, seems
to have been caught in the tide that led ultimately to stage realism
as we know it today, for it is apparent that Latrobe's theater was
designed without proscenium doors.

On May 25, 1820, "between the hours of 1 and 2 this morning,"
the Park Theater burned to the ground.[25] A new building of somewhat the same character was erected on the site, and like the
earlier structure it too burned in 1848.[26] Several years later work-
men engaged in clearing away the ruins of the second Park dis-

142

covered the cornerstone of the original theater. The stone was given to Edward Windust, the proprietor of a restaurant a few doors west of the theater lot.[27] Out of affection for the old building, or a sense of history (or more than likely because it was a conversation piece), Windust fixed the stone to the wall of his restaurant, where it stood for many years, the only reminder of what may well have been America's greatest eighteenth-century playhouse.[28]

Perhaps the most important architectural effort of the late eighteenth century (at least on paper) was Benjamin Latrobe's set of designs for a building to replace Quesnay's Academy at Richmond. The designs were commissioned by the theatrical manager Thomas Wade West.[29] Latrobe states that they were begun on December 2, 1797, and completed on January 8, 1798.[30] Containing a hotel and various public rooms as well as a theater, the proposed building was unique. The brick structure, the central portion of which contained the theater, was to have been 148 feet 8 inches in total width and 104 feet in depth (Fig. 45). Designed with Roman architecture in mind—or at least such works as Palladio's in which Roman types were shown—it possessed a monumental facade and starkly simple arched loggia that relate it in some degree to such contemporary English theaters as James Wyatt's Theater Royal, Birmingham, of 1795, and to later American buildings like William Strickland's second Chestnut Street Theater of 1822. But it is clear that Latrobe's building, had it been completed, would have been far more handsome than either of these structures, and indeed a better house than anything ever seen in England aside from the great theaters of London.

Although the exterior of the proposed theater and hotel is evidently original work, the auditorium seems to indicate that Latrobe may also have been influenced to a degree by the James Lewis designs for a theater at Limerick (Figs. 46–52). The audi-

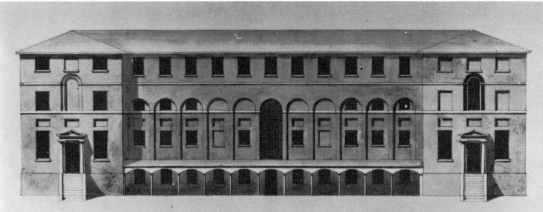

Elevation of the South-East FRONT.

Elevation of the PRINCIPAL, a N. West, FRONT.

45 / Elevation of the southeast front (top) and northwest front (bottom) of Benjamin Latrobe's proposed Richmond, Virginia, theater. Watercolor by Latrobe, 1798.

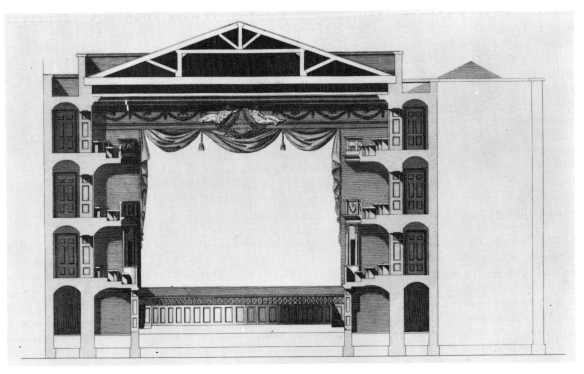

46 / Limerick Theater, section of the auditorium. Drawing by James Lewis, 1788.

toriums of both houses are semi-circular, and somewhat wider and more shallow than those found in earlier theaters; and although columns appear at various places in Latrobe's theater, the two upper tiers of side boxes are cantilevered like those in Lewis' designs. Although the proposed Richmond house contained a dome over the pit not seen at Limerick, the overall character of the two auditoriums was similar, and, in some cases, the detail work at Richmond might well have been directly adapted from the designs for the Irish theater. Thus, while absolute evidence is lacking for an attribution of Latrobe's house to that at Limerick, a resemblance may readily be detected.

145

47 / Section of Latrobe's proposed Richmond theater, 1798.

48 / The front boxes, Latrobe's proposed Richmond theater, 1798.

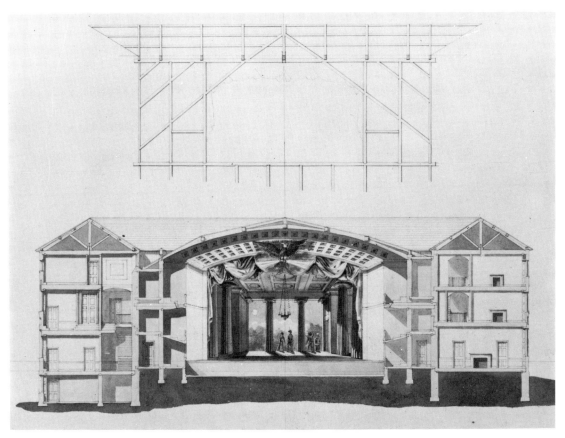

49 / The stage, Latrobe's proposed Richmond theater, 1798.

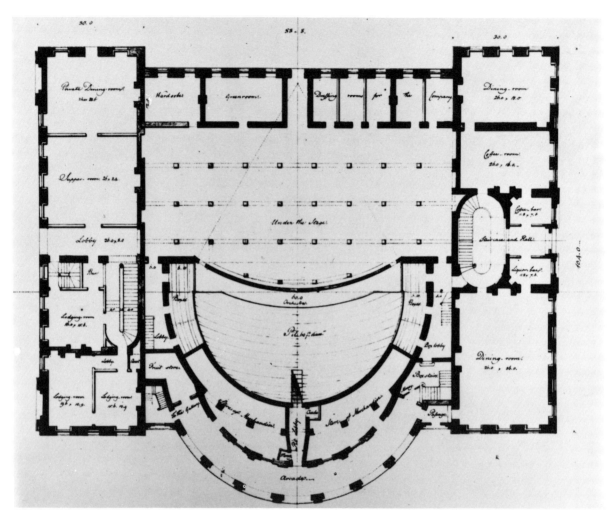

50 / Plan of the ground floor, Latrobe's proposed Richmond theater, 1798.

148

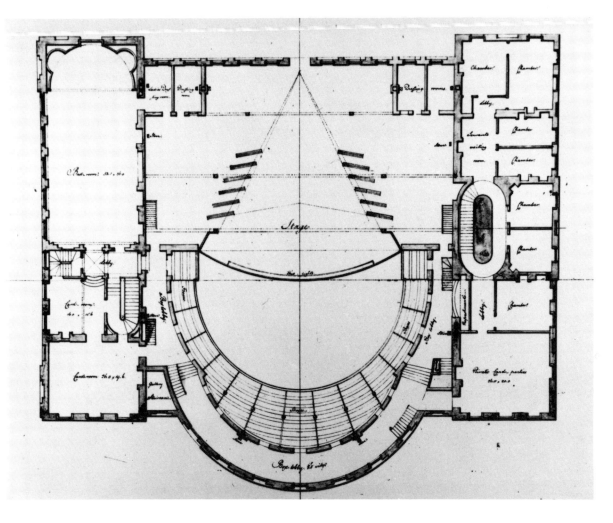

51 / Plan of the first floor, Latrobe's proposed Richmond theater, 1798.

149

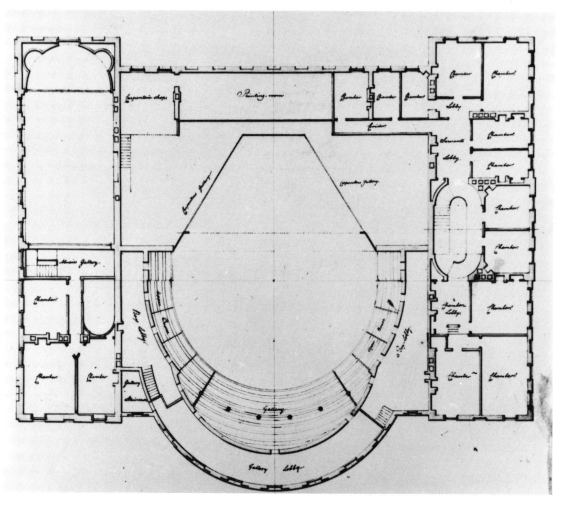

52 / Plan of the second floor, Latrobe's proposed Richmond theater, 1798.

Perhaps the most important feature of Latrobe's theater, how ever, does not appear at the playhouse that Lewis designed. At the contemplated Richmond theater, pit passages had been done away with entirely and entrance to the pit was from the rear center of the auditorium (Fig. 50). As in many modern theaters, a flight of stairs led directly up into the pit from the lobby, but the flight of steps did not lead to a central aisle. Instead it stopped short a little less than half of the way back in the pit, and the spectators presumably were to walk down to their seats over the tops of the benches. No similar arrangement has been located in any other British or American theater, though British precedents for a somewhat similar plan do exist: as early as 1743, Dublin's Fishamble Street Theater contained an entrance to the pit at the rear of the auditorium and an actual aisle down the center of the pit to the orchestra;[31] in 1798 the Crow Street Theater in the same city was remodeled to include aisles, both in the center and at the sides of the auditorium, that could be covered by hinged flaps to provide additional seating on a crowded night.[32] The central aisle that Latrobe's auditorium anticipates, uncommon in the eighteenth century, became the common entrance system in many English and American theaters in the early years of the nineteenth century. Even more than the Park, then, Latrobe's playhouse designed for Richmond marked the first steps toward a new era in auditorium design.[33]

The absence of proscenium doors in Latrobe's plans and drawings seems curious. That the architect merely omitted them from his sketches for some unknown reason seems extremely unlikely since Latrobe's portfolio lays out the theater in extraordinary detail. It is more reasonable to suppose that the design of the stage for the contemplated Richmond theater was as much in advance of its time as the auditorium, for other elements of the stagehouse are far more characteristic of nineteenth-century houses than of those found in England and America in the 1780's and 1790's.[34]

151

Certain details of Latrobe's stage, however, are not untypical of conventional houses of the time: the usual forestage may still been seen; the stage is raked slightly from front to back; and the scenery is constructed in artificial perspective. In other respects, Latrobe's playhouse approaches the theaters of the Victorian period: the absence of proscenium doors and the raking of the stage wings shown in the plans and sketches, for example, are extraordinarily unconventional for so early a building, and the proscenium opening (more than fifty feet) is far wider than that seen at most eighteenth-century playhouses.

Although it is difficult to determine exactly, it is probable that Latrobe intended the scenery in his theater to be shifted by the English groove system. Admittedly the use of grooves would have been difficult where raked sets of wings were employed, but the combination of sloping stage floor and raked wings was to be found in some later English theaters.[35] The conventional fly floor or carpenter's gallery found in Latrobe's plans suggests even more strongly that some variation of the groove system was definitely in use at the theater, and there is a possible indication of upper grooves to be seen on the first three downstage left sets of wings in the plan of the first floor of the playhouse (Fig. 51).[36]

Perhaps the contemplated Richmond theater was not to be so lavishly furnished with stage machinery as New York's Park Theater, but it is impossible to tell, for Latrobe omitted from his plans and drawings any equipment that was not part of the actual fabric of the building. Yet the comparatively generous use of space behind the proscenium arch—with a green room, no less than nine dressing rooms, a costume room, a carpenter shop, and even a counterweighted scene painter's frame—demonstrates that the backstage facilities at the Richmond building would have been far superior to those at the Chestnut Street Theater as it was remodeled and enlarged in the early nineteenth century.

Indeed, although it was a smaller house, the Richmond theater

53 / Contemporary architect's model based on Benjamin Latrobe's plans for the Richmond theater.

would have contained backstage space almost as good as that to be found at London's Covent Garden.[37]

Thus, in the design of the stage as well as the auditorium, the proposed Richmond playhouse illustrates both a transition to the theater of the nineteenth century and the highest point of American theater architecture in its day. Latrobe had carefully considered the requirements for an ideal theater to house the new drama of the late eighteenth century. That drama was marked by an increasing illusionism and a tendency toward spectacular display, and Latrobe had provided all of the physical facilities necessary to the implementation of the most contemporary dramatic forms. Latrobe's plan is both spacious and efficiently arranged, and in concept, if not in time, far more than half a century removed from the stages of the first English managers in America.

Since 1959, the city of Richmond has recognized the need for a legitimate theater in the downtown area. In the summer of 1964, a group of Richmond citizens banded together to impress upon the city the need for such a facility and the desirability of using Latrobe's designs. As these chapters are being written, it seems likely that the playhouse will finally be erected on a site not far from the original location chosen by Latrobe himself. In the present plans for the structure, the stage will be redesigned for modern theatrical productions, and Latrobe's scheme for the auditorium will be slightly modified; however, the exterior of the building (Fig. 53) will be virtually unchanged. Ironically, more than a century and a half after Latrobe's plans were drawn, Richmond may at last possess one of the architect's finest projects—and the only eighteenth-century playhouse in America.

Notes / Index

Notes

I. THE AMATEUR PERIOD

1. Ralph T. Whitelaw, *Virginia's Eastern Shore* (Richmond: Virginia Historical Society, 1951), I, 708–715; Louis B. Wright, *The Cultural Life of the American Colonies, 1607–1763* (New York: Harper and Row, 1957), pp. 178–179.

2. George C. D. Odell, *Annals of the New York Stage* (New York: Columbia University Press, 1927–1949), I, 21. Some writers believe Holt's pantomime was a puppet production, although there is as much reason to believe that live actors appeared in it. Cf. Paul McPharlin, *The Puppet Theatre in America* (New York: Harper and Bros., 1949), p. 39. Ada Louise Huxtable, *Classic New York* (Garden City, N.Y.: Doubleday and Co., 1964), pp. 6–8, points out that the De Lancey house, now known as Fraunces Tavern, is a "scholarly fake." It is, therefore, impossible to determine anything about the circumstances of Holt's production from the present building.

3. Odell, *Annals,* I, 11–12.

4. Thomas Allston Brown, *A History of the New York Stage* (New York: Dodd, Mead and Co., 1903), I, 1.

5. New York *Weekly Journal,* August 28, 1749. An earlier advertisement (New York *Weekly Journal,* July 24, 1749) mentions front seats, middle gallery, and upper gallery. Presumably the middle and upper galleries were only slightly elevated portions of the pit.

6. Thomas Clark Pollock, *The Philadelphia Theatre in the Eighteenth Century* (Philadelphia: University of Pennsylvania Press, 1933), pp. 4–5.

7. See Sybil Rosenfeld, *The Theatre of the London Fairs in the 18th Century* (Cambridge, Eng.: Cambridge University Press, 1960), pp. 150–169.

8. *York County Records, Orders, Wills, Book XV,* quoted in Mary A.

Stephenson, "The First Theatre," Manuscript Report in the Department of Research, Colonial Williamsburg, Williamsburg, Virginia, Illustration IA, 1946.

9. *Ibid.*

10. James W. Knight, "Archaeological Report, Block 29, Area G (Northwest Corner of Colonial Lot 164), October, 1947," Manuscript Report in the Department of Research, Colonial Williamsburg, Williamsburg, Virginia, p. 3.

11. *Virginia Gazette* (Williamsburg), December 19, 1745.

12. Arnold Hare, *The Georgian Theatre in Wessex* (London: Phoenix House, 1958), pp. 127–137.

13. Edward A. Langhans, "Wren's Restoration Playhouse," *Theatre Notebook,* XVIII (Spring 1964), 91–100.

14. *South Carolina Gazette* (Charleston), January 24, 1736.

15. *Architectural Record,* LXXXIII (January 1938), 20–25.

II. PROFESSIONAL BEGINNINGS

1. Quoted in Hugh F. Rankin, *The Theater in Colonial America* (Chapel Hill: University of North Carolina Press, 1965), p. 50.

2. Pollock, *Philadelphia Theatre,* p. 6.

3. New York *Weekly Post-Boy,* February 26, 1750.

4. Quoted in William Dunlap, *History of the American Theatre,* Burt Franklin Research and Source Works Series, No. 36 (New York: Burt Franklin, 1963), I, 353–354.

5. New York *Weekly Post-Boy,* January 21, 1751.

6. Joseph N. Ireland, *Records of the New York Stage, from 1759 to 1860* (New York: T. H. Norrell, 1866), I, 16.

7. For a complete record of the theater see Mary A. Stephenson, "The Second Theatre," Manuscript Report in the Department of Research, Colonial Williamsburg, Williamsburg, Virginia, 1946.

8. *Virginia Gazette* (Williamsburg), August 21, 1752.

9. Rankin, *Theater,* p. 38.

10. Paul Leicester Ford, *Washington and the Theatre* (New York: The Dunlap Society, 1899), p. 9.

11. Dunlap, *American Theatre,* I, 22.

12. *Maryland Gazette* (Annapolis), December 7, 1752.

13. Andrew Burnaby, *Travels Through the Middle Settlements in*

North America, in the Years 1759 and 1760 (London: printed for T. Payne, 1775), p. 38.

14. Letter Book, 1752, Dr. George Gilmer, from a manuscript copy made by Dr. Robert A. Brock in the Department of Research, Colonial Williamsburg, Williamsburg, Virginia; *Virginia Gazette* (Williamsburg), August 21, 1752.

15. *Virginia Gazette* (Williamsburg), August 28, 1752.

16. *Maryland Gazette* (Annapolis), September 6, 1770.

17. Dunlap, *American Theatre,* I, 15.

18. Original playbills, Second Theater, Department of Research, Colonial Williamsburg, Williamsburg, Virginia.

19. *Virginia Gazette* (Williamsburg), August 21, 1752.

20. Charles Beecher Hogan, "The New Wells, Goodman's Fields, 1739–1752," *Theatre Notebook,* III (July–September 1949), 67–72.

21. *York County Records, Orders, Wills, Book XV,* quoted in Stephenson, "The First Theatre," Illustration IA.

22. *Virginia Gazette* (Williamsburg), December 8, 1752.

23. See correspondence between Singleton Moorehead and Richard Southern, April 1953, in the Department of Architecture, Colonial Williamsburg, Williamsburg, Virginia.

24. Stephenson, "The Second Theatre," p. 26.

25. For a detailed study of the Hallam tour, see Rankin, *Theater,* pp. 60–73.

26. Dunlap, *American Theatre,* I, 32.

27. *Ibid.*

28. New York *Mercury,* January 8, 1759; *Pennsylvania Gazette* (Philadelphia), June 27, 1754; John F. Watson, ed., *Annals of Philadelphia and Pennsylvania in the Olden Time* (Philadelphia, n.p., 1844), I, 472.

29. Quoted in Odell, *Annals,* I, 56.

30. New York *Weekly Post-Boy,* September 17, 1753.

31. Quoted in Odell, *Annals,* I, 58.

32. Montague Summers, *The Restoration Theatre* (New York: Macmillan, 1934), pp. 97, 164.

33. Richard Southern, *Changeable Scenery* (London: Faber and Faber, 1952), p. 172, illustrates a nineteenth-century curtain of the bottom roller type. The rigging and construction of the curtain are very similar to that shown in modern stagecraft texts.

34. Brown, *New York Stage,* I, 5.

III. THE RISE OF DAVID DOUGLASS

1. Richardson Wright, *Revels in Jamaica* (New York: Dodd, Mead and Co., 1937), pp. 6, 41–42; Ruth Crosby Dimmick, *Our Theatres Today and Yesterday* (New York: H. K. Fly Co., 1913), p. 13.
2. Watson, ed., *Annals of Pennsylvania*, I, 472.
3. Pollock, *Philadelphia Theatre*, pp. 14–15.
4. Pennsylvania Archives, Ser. III, 659–660, quoted in Richard D. Stine, "The Philadelphia Theatre, 1682–1829: Its Growth as a Cultural Institution" (unpub. diss., University of Pennsylvania, 1951), p. 31.
5. New York *Mercury*, December 28, 1761.
6. George O. Seilhamer, *History of the American Theatre* (Philadelphia: Globe Printing House, 1888), I, 113; William Eddis, *Letters from America* (London: C. Dilly, 1792), p. 93.
7. George O. Willard, *History of the Providence Stage*, 1762–1891 (Providence: Rhode Island News Company, 1891), p. 6.
8. See Odell, *Annals*, I, 93–95.
9. New York *Gazette*, April 12, 1764.
10. New York *Mercury*, February 1, 1762; December 28, 1761.
11. *Ibid.*, January 4, 1762; March 8, 1762.
12. Undated article concerning the Richmond, Virginia, theater fire of 1811, presumably from a Richmond newspaper, in the Harvard Theatre Collection.
13. *Pennsylvania Gazette* (Philadelphia), December 16, 1772.
14. New York *Post-Boy*, December 31, 1761; January 11, 1762.
15. *South Carolina Gazette* (Charleston), November 5, 1763.
16. Willard, *Providence Stage*, p. 12.

IV. THE SOUTHWARK AND JOHN STREET

1. Pollock, *Philadelphia Theatre*, p. 19.
2. Stine, "Philadelphia Theatre," pp. 39–40; Charles Durang, *The Philadelphia Stage: From 1749 to 1821*, Series I, which ran serially in the Philadelphia *Sunday Dispatch*, May 7, 1854, to June 29, 1854, Chap. III.
3. *Ibid.*, Series I, I.
4. *Pennsylvania Journal* (Philadelphia), June 11, 1767.

5. Durang, Series I, Chap. I.

6. *Ibid.*

7. Dunlap, *American Theatre,* I, 51.

8. Royall Tyler, *The Contrast,* in Arthur Hobson Quinn, ed., *Representative American Plays* (New York: Appleton-Century-Crofts, 1957), p. 64.

9. Dunlap, *American Theatre,* I, 51.

10. *Ibid.*

11. Odell, *Annals,* I, 328, 329.

12. Watson, ed., *Annals of Pennsylvania,* I, 473.

13. Stine, "Philadelphia Theatre," p. 27; Alan S. Downer, ed., *The Memoir of John Durang, American Actor, 1785–1816* (Pittsburgh: University of Pittsburgh Press, 1966), p. 23.

14. *Theatre Royal Account Book,* February 27, 1779.

15. New York *Weekly Post-Boy,* November 19, 1750.

16. New York *Mercury,* February 1, 1762.

17. Charles Durang, Series I, Chap. XIV.

18. Quoted in Richard Southern, *The Georgian Playhouse* (London: Pleides Books, 1948), p. 25.

19. See Martin Holmes and William Van Lennep, "Westminster and the USA," *Theatre Notebook,* IV (July–September 1950), 85–88.

20. *South Carolina Gazette* (Charleston), October 30, 1766.

21. Cf. Arthur Hornblow, *A History of the Theatre in America from Its Beginnings to the Present Time* (Philadelphia: J. B. Lippincott Co., 1919), p. 142.

22. *Maryland Gazette* (Annapolis), September 3, 1772.

23. Royall Tyler, *The Contrast,* in Quinn, ed., *Representative American Plays,* p. 65.

24. William Dunlap, *Diary* (New York: New York Historical Society, 1929), p. 142.

25. Quoted in Odell, *Annals,* I, 88.

26. Quoted *ibid.,* I, 165.

27. Thomas Godfrey, *The Prince of Parthia,* in Quinn, ed., *Representative American Plays,* p. 13.

28. Dunlap, *American Theatre,* I, 51.

29. W. J. Lawrence, "Early American Playgoing," *The Theatre,* XXIV (December 1916), 404.

30. See H. P. Phelps, *Players of a Century: A Record of the Albany Stage* (Albany: Joseph McDonough, 1880), p. 19; C. J. Sauthier, *Plan of*

the Town of Halifax in Halifax County North Carolina, Survey'd & Drawn in June 1769 by C. J. Sauthier (copy in the Department of Architecture, Colonial Williamsburg, Williamsburg, Virginia); J. Thomas Scharf, *The Chronicles of Baltimore* (Baltimore: Turnbull Bros., 1874), pp. 112–113; Edward A. Wyatt, "Three Petersburg Theatres," *William and Mary Quarterly*, Series II, XXI (April 1941), 84; Thomas B. Rowland, "Norfolk Theatres of the Olden Time," *The Lower Norfolk County Virginia Antiquary*, II (1898), 102.

31. Durang, Series I, Chap. I.

32. *Ibid.*

V. TOWN AND COUNTRY THEATERS
AFTER THE REVOLUTION

1. Quoted in Barnard Hewitt, *Theatre U.S.A., 1665 to 1957* (New York: McGraw-Hill, 1959), p. 30.

2. Dunlap, *American Theatre*, I, 246–248; Frank Chouteau Brown, "The First Boston Theatre, on Federal Street," *Old-Time New England*, XXXVI (July 1945), 1. Although Dunlap speaks of the building as specifically erected for theatrical production, Brown indicates that the playhouse was a former stable.

3. Quoted *ibid.*

4. Prologue by Mitchell Sewall, quoted in Seilhamer, *History of American Theatre*, III, 14.

5. James Moreland, "The Theatre in Portland in the Eighteenth Century," *The New England Quarterly*, II (June 1938), 333–334.

6. See Edward Garland Fletcher, "Records and History of Theatrical Activities in Pittsburgh, Pennsylvania, from their Beginning to 1861" (unpub. diss. Harvard University, 1931), I, 1–3; George W. Ranck, *History of Lexington, Kentucky* (Cincinnati: Roger Clarke and Co., 1872), p. 203; Alonzo Thomas Dill, *Governor Tryon and His Palace* (Chapel Hill: University of North Carolina Press, 1955), pp. 232–233.

7. Martin Staples Shockley, "The Richmond Theatre, 1780–1790," *The Virginia Magazine of History and Biography*, LX (July 1952), 424; Samuel Mordecai, *Virginia, Especially Richmond, in By-Gone Days* (Richmond: West and Johnson, 1860), p. 198.

8. Quoted in Scharf, *Chronicles of Baltimore*, p. 114.

9. Nelly Custis to Elizabeth Bordley, March 20, 1798. The original

letter is owned by the Mount Vernon Ladies Association of the Union. A copy may be seen in the files of the Department of Architecture, Colonial Williamsburg, Williamsburg, Virginia.

10. Seilhamer, *History of American Theatre,* II, 53.

11. Scharf, *Chronicles of Baltimore,* p. 113; O. G. Sonneck, *Early Opera in America* (New York: G. Shirmer, 1915), p. 60.

12. Cf. Rankin, *Theater,* 43–188.

13. Eola Willis, *The Charleston Stage in the XVIII Century* (Columbia, S. C.: The State Company, 1924), p. 104.

14. Charleston *Morning Post,* June 30, 1786.

15. *Ibid.,* July 14, 1786.

16. New York *Independent Journal,* August 5, 1786.

17. George Saunders, *A Treatise on Theatres* (London: J. and J. Taylor, 1790), p. 83.

18. Seilhamer, *History of American Theatre,* II, 161.

19. *Ibid.*

20. Suzanne Ketchum Sherman, "Thomas Wade West, Theatrical Impresario, 1790–1799," *William and Mary Quarterly,* VIII (July 1951), 11–33; Seilhamer, *History of American Theatre,* II, 204.

21. Sherman, "Thomas Wade West," p. 27.

22. René J. Le Gardeur, Jr., *The First New Orleans Theatre, 1792–1803* (New Orleans: Leeward Books, 1963), pp. 2–3.

23. *Ibid.,* p. 9.

24. Both Mr. Le Gardeur and Mr. Samuel Wilson, an authority on the early architecture of New Orleans, have informed the writer that no authentic illustration of *Le Spectacle* is known to exist.

25. Antoinette F. Downing and Vincent J. Scully, Jr., *The Architectural History of Newport, Rhode Island* (Cambridge: Harvard University Press, 1952), pp. 77–78; Willard, *Providence Stage,* p. 23.

26. Willis, *The Charleston Stage,* p. 237.

27. *Ibid.*

VI. THE THEATERS OF THOMAS WADE WEST

1. Cf. Talbot Hamlin, *The American Spirit in Architecture* (New Haven: Yale University Press, 1926), pp. 109, 120.

2. Quoted in Willard, *Providence Stage,* p. 114.

3. *New York Magazine,* September 1792.

4. Unidentified newspaper article, p. 17, Fred G. Ross scrapbook, Theatre Collection, Lincoln Center for the Performing Arts.

5. Charleston, *City Gazette and Daily Advertiser,* February 13, 1793.

6. Quoted in Willis, *The Charleston Stage,* pp. 260–261.

7. Quoted *ibid.,* p. 224.

8. Sherman, "Thomas Wade West," p. 18.

9. *Ibid.*

10. *Ibid.,* p. 24.

11. *Ibid.,* p. 18.

12. Rowland, "Norfolk Theaters," p. 103.

13. *Ibid.*

14. Sherman, "Thomas Wade West," p. 24.

15. Wyatt, "Three Petersburg Theatres," p. 88.

16. *Ibid.,* pp. 88–89.

17. *Ibid.,* p. 89.

18. Sherman, "Thomas Wade West," p. 24.

19. Wyatt, "Three Petersburg Theatres," p. 89.

20. Seilhamer, *History of American Theatre,* II, 70.

21. Willard, *Providence Stage,* p. 24.

22. *Ibid.,* p. 25.

23. *Ibid.*

24. *Ibid.*

25. *Ibid.,* pp. 25–26; Wyatt, "Three Petersburg Theatres," pp. 88–89.

26. Cf. Wyatt, "Three Petersburg Theatres," p. 90.

27. Willard, *Providence Stage,* p. 26.

28. Cf. Southern, *The Georgian Playhouse,* Plate 33.

29. Cf. Willard, *Providence Stage,* pp. 26, 75.

30. Cf. Southern, *The Georgian Playhouse,* Plates 3 and 4.

31. Southern, *Changeable Scenery,* p. 168.

32. Willard, *Providence Stage,* p. 26.

33. A number of later nineteenth-century stage curtains are still in existence. One interesting example of a painted act curtain that is not generally known to exist is from the Swedish communist colony at Bishop Hill, Illinois, and is preserved in the museum there.

34. Cf. Willard, *Providence Stage,* p. 112.

35. For a discussion of the working mechanism of traps in the eighteenth century see Phyllis Hartnoll, ed., *The Oxford Companion to the Theatre* (London: Oxford University Press, 1962), pp. 242–243.

36. Quoted in Willis, *The Charleston Stage,* p. 143.

37. Norfolk *Herald and Public Advertiser,* July 8, 1797.

38. Quoted in Odell, *Annals,* I, 256.

39. Hartnoll, ed., *Oxford Companion,* p. 483.

40. *Virginia Gazette and Petersburg Intelligencer* (Petersburg), February 28, 1797.

41. Quoted in Seilhamer, *History of American Theatre,* II, 166–167.

42. Cf. Hartnoll, ed., *Oxford Companion,* p. 242.

43. Norfolk *Herald and Public Advertiser,* June 10, 1798.

44. *Ibid.,* July 8, 1797.

45. *Virginia Gazette and General Advertiser* (Richmond), December 16, 1791; cf. *Charleston City Gazette and Daily Advertiser,* April 20, 1793.

46. *Virginia Gazette and General Advertiser* (Richmond), December 16, 1791.

47. *Ibid.*

48. New York *Daily Advertiser,* April 4, 1787.

49. Norfolk *Herald and Public Advertiser,* June 8, 1802.

50. The following theaters, many of them of a more or less temporary nature, were in use between 1798 and 1800: the theater at Detroit, Michigan, 1798; the theater at Washington Hall, Salem, Massachusetts, 1799; the theater in Mrs. Suter's Long Room, Georgetown, 1799 (a photograph of the building may be found in the Library of Congress Print Room); The Six Buildings, Washington, D.C., 1799 (photograph in the Library of Congress Print Room); the theater at Washington, D.C., 1800 (a former residence; a print of the building is in the Library of Congress Print Room); and the Summer Theater at Mount Vernon Gardens, New York, 1800.

51. Nelly Custis to Elizabeth Bordley, March 20, 1798.

52. *Columbian Mirror and Alexandria Gazette* (Alexandria), November 6, 1793.

53. Sherman, "Thomas Wade West," p. 27.

54. *Virginia Gazette and Petersburg Intelligencer* (Petersburg), February 3, 1797.

55. *Ibid.*

56. Mary G. Powell, *History of Old Alexandria, Virginia* (Richmond: n.p., 1928), p. 143.

57. Wilhelmus Bogart Bryan, *History of the National Capitol* (New York: MacMillan, 1914), I, 334.

58. Unidentified newspaper article, p. 17, Fred G. Ross scrapbook, Theatre Collection, Lincoln Center for the Performing Arts.

VII. CHESTNUT STREET, FEDERAL STREET, AND THE
HAYMARKET

1. Quoted in David McNeely Stauffer, ed., *Westcott's History of Philadelphia* (Philadelphia: n.p., 1913), XVII, 1263.
2. Seilhamer, *History of American Theatre,* II, 177.
3. Stauffer, ed., *Westcott's History,* XVII, 1264.
4. William Thornton papers, Library of Congress, Washington, D.C.
5. *American Monthly Magazine,* September 1828.
6. Until recently it was believed that Benjamin Henry Latrobe designed the Chestnut Street Theater. Cf. Henri Marceau, *William Rush, 1756–1833, the First American Sculptor* (Philadelphia: n.p., 1937), p. 24; Stine, "Philadelphia Theatre," p. 110. A recent doctoral dissertation, however, has disproved this theory, demonstrating that Latrobe was not the original architect of the structure. See Abe Wollock, "Benjamin Henry Latrobe's Activities in the American Theatre (1797–1808)" (unpub. diss., University of Illinois, 1962).
7. Charles Durang, Series I, Chap. I.
8. Philadelphia *American Daily Advertiser,* April 5, 1820.
9. Pollock, *Philadelphia Theatre,* p. 55.
10. Quoted in Stine, "Philadelphia Theatre," p. 113. In the same passage, Saint-Méry indicates that the theater seated 1,250. Stine believes that the building when completed seated 2,000 persons, although he gives no source for his statement.
11. Stauffer, ed., *Westcott's History,* XVII, 1265.
12. These statues were evidently Rush's first commission. They survived the fire of 1820 and were placed in niches in the second Chestnut Street Theater. They may be seen in the engraving of the second theater reproduced in Oral Sumner Coad and Edwin Mims, Jr., *The American Stage* (New Haven: Yale University Press, 1929), p. 82.
13. Quoted in Charles Durang, Series I, Chap. I.
14. Charles Durang, Series I, Chap. II. The only surviving view of the early auditorium of the Bath theater is reproduced in Southern, *The Georgian Playhouse,* Plate 15.
15. Cf. Southern, *The Georgian Playhouse,* p. 32.
16. *Ibid.,* pp. 33–34.
17. Wollock, "Latrobe's Activities," p. 83.
18. Wollock does not reproduce this plan or comment on it. Stine, however, writing some years before Wollock, correctly identifies it as a

plan of the first Chestnut Street Theater rather than the second building erected on the site, as had previously been stated by writers on the subject. There is no doubt that Etins is correct, for the plan corresponds in every particular to the views of the Chestnut Street facade after its remodeling by Latrobe. It is even possible roughly to date the plan since a structure labeled "Gas House" is shown, and it is known that the theater was not adapted for gas until a few years before its destruction by fire in 1820.

19. Quoted in Sonneck, *Early Opera*, p. 113.

20. Quoted *ibid.*, pp. 119–120. Lord Barrymore was a well-known English theatrical amateur with private theaters in both his London residence and his country house at Wargrave. The scenery may have been purchased second-hand by Richards and shipped to Wignell for temporary use.

21. Quoted *ibid.*, p. 115.

22. Quoted in Hewitt, *Theatre U.S.A.*, pp. 39–40.

23. Latrobe's alterations are discussed at length in Wollock. "Latrobe's Activities," pp. 36ff.

24. Philadelphia *American Daily Advertiser*, April 3, 1820.

25. The statues are owned by the Edwin Forrest Home, Philadelphia.

26. Pollock, *Philadelphia Theatre*, pp. 58–59, 63–64, 66.

27. Downer, ed., *John Durang,* 69–70.

28. Pollock, *Philadelphia Theatre,* p. 64.

29. Quoted in Hornblow, *Theatre in America*, p. 241; F. C. Brown, "The First Boston Theatre," p. 4.

30. John Alden, "A Season in Federal Street," *Proceedings of the American Antiquarian Society* (1955), p. 11. Alden says that the theater had been originally estimated to cost $17,500, but that the final figure was close to $40,000. William J. Clapp, Jr., *A Record of the Boston Stage* (Boston: J. Munroe and Co., 1853), p. 59, says that the building cost $70,000.

31. F. C. Brown, "The First Boston Theatre," p. 4.

32. Some of the variations in the placement of doors to boxes, pit, and gallery may be observed in Southern's *The Georgian Playhouse* and in the famous Woodfall prints of English theaters, copies of which may be seen in the Harvard Theatre Collection. It is known that the pit door at Federal Street was located on the north side of the building after its reconstruction in 1798, since that entrance, clearly labeled, may be seen in surviving prints of the building.

167

33. Clapp, *Record of the Boston Stage,* pp. 19–20.

34. F. C. Brown, "The First Boston Theatre," p. 5.

35. *Ibid.,* p. 4.

36. *Ibid.,* p. 6.

37. Alden, "A Season in Federal Street," p. 31.

38. Cf. F. C. Brown, "The First Boston Theatre," p. 6.

39. Clapp, *Record of the Boston Stage,* pp. 19–20.

40. Alden, "A Season in Federal Street," p. 12, lists their price as £37 16s. 10d.

41. *Ibid.*

42. *Ibid.*

43. F. C. Brown, "The First Boston Theatre," pp. 6–7.

44. *Ibid.*

45. Southern, *The Georgian Playhouse,* pp. 33–34.

46. New York *Commercial Advertiser,* January 31, 1798.

47. Hartnoll, ed., *Oxford Companion,* p. 203.

48. Alden, "A Season in Federal Street," pp. 17–18.

49. Quoted *ibid.,* p. 26.

50. Odell, *Annals,* II, 60.

51. Seilhamer, *History of American Theatre,* III, 354.

52. Dunlap, *American Theatre,* I, 273.

53. *Ibid.,* 273–274.

54. Quoted *ibid.,* 313–314.

55. The frontispiece to Brackenridge's play is reproduced in Coad and Mims, *American Stage,* p. 23.

VIII. THE PARK AND THE PROPOSED RICHMOND THEATER

1. Odell, *Annals,* II, 1.

2. *Ibid.,* 2.

3. *Ibid.,* 5.

4. Ireland, *Records of the New York Stage,* I, 12.

5. T. B. Thorpe, "The Old Theatres of New York, 1750–1827," *Appleton's Journal,* VIII (November 23, 1872), 578.

6. Richard Beamish, *Memoir of the Life of Sir Marc Isambard Brunel* (London: Longman, Green, Longman and Bros., 1862), p. 33.

7. New York *Daily Advertiser,* January 31, 1798.

8. Hamlin, *The American Spirit in Architecture,* p. 106.

9. Ireland, *Records of the New York Stage,* I, 11; New York *Daily Advertiser,* January 31, 1798.

10. New York *Commercial Advertiser,* January 31, 1798.

11. Dunlap, *American Theatre,* II, 247.

12. Cf. Figs. 32 and 44. A cross section of the Limerick Theater showing the cantilevered boxes appears in Southern, *The Georgian Playhouse,* Fig. 8.

13. Odell, *Annals,* II, 25, 26, 172, 551–563.

14. Two views of the new Park Theater that was erected on the site of the first building after its destruction by fire are extant. They represent the auditorium in 1821 and 1822 and do not, as some writers have suggested, show the interior of the first Park Theater of 1798. Both views are reproduced in Coad and Mims, *American Stage,* pp. 52, 78.

15. Washington Irving, in Montrose Moses and John Mason Brown, eds., *The American Theatre as Seen by Its Critics, 1752–1934* (New York: W. W. Norton and Co., 1934), pp. 46–47.

16. Odell, *Annals,* II, 25.

17. *Ibid.,* pp. 25–26.

18. For a discussion of the transitional period in English auditorium design see Southern, *The Georgian Playhouse,* pp. 54–62.

19. New York *Commercial Advertiser,* January 31, 1798.

20. *Ibid.*

21. Washington Irving, in Moses and Brown, eds., *The American Theatre,* p. 43.

22. Odell, *Annals,* II, is in large part devoted to the operation of the Park Theater. In the volume are to be found some fifty descriptions of the scenery and machinery in use at the theater. Of special interest is his treatment of staging, pp. 223–226.

23. For the complete text of this and the two following advertisements see Odell, II, 56–60.

24. Cf. *Ibid,* 223–225.

25. *Ibid.,* 563.

26. Ireland, *Records of the New York Stage,* I, 69.

27. *Ibid.*

28. *Ibid.*

29. Sherman, "Thomas Wade West," pp. 24–25.

30. Benjamin Henry Latrobe, "Designs of a Building Proposed to be Erected at Richmond in Virginia, to Contain a Theatre, Assembly-

Rooms, and an Hotel," architectural portfolio, Library of Congress, title page.

31. A print of the Fishamble Street playhouse that shows the center aisle is preserved in the collection of the Department of Research, Colonial Williamsburg. La Tourette Stockwell, *Dublin Theatre and Theatre Customs, 1637–1820* (Kingsport, Tenn.: n.p., 1938), p. 162.

32. *Ibid.,* p. 159

33. For more detailed discussion of the interior of the proposed Richmond playhouse see Talbot Hamlin, *Benjamin Henry Latrobe* (New York: Oxford University Press, 1955), pp. 117–120; Wollock, "Latrobe's Activities," pp. 70ff.

34. For a brief study of early nineteenth-century English theaters see Southern, *The Georgian Playhouse*, pp. 54–62.

35. Cf. Southern, *Changeable Scenery*, pp. 88–90.

36. It is possible that a somewhat similar carpenter's gallery existed at Chestnut Street, although the broken lines seen in the plan of that building may represent the vanishing lines for the stage wings.

37. Cf. Southern, *The Georgian Playhouse*, p. 22.

Index

174

From the construction of the first crude playhouse at Williamsburg, Virginia, about 1716, to the completion of New York's splendid Park Theater in 1798, more than seventy playhouses were built in America. Though none of these theaters still stands, Brooks McNamara has explored every possible clue — playbills, ground plans, newspapers, manuscripts, prints and drawings, diaries, fragments of stage equipment and walls—to put together this first architectural history of the eighteenth-century American playhouse. He traces the extensive influence of English stagecraft and theater architecture on the evolution of the American playhouse, discussing the dominance of English acting companies from mid-century to the Revolution and the resurgence and refinement of theater building in the later years of the century.

Perceptively portraying the flavor and spectacle of eighteenth-century theater, Mr. McNamara vividly recreates the settings of early American dramatic performances. To the audiences of the time "the more obviously 'theatrical' a setting, the better . . . The very changing of the scenes in front of the spectator's eyes, for example, was considered almost as much a part of an evening at the theater as the play itself, and every scenic tour de force possible was incorporated in the plays and after-pieces." The mechanics of such tours de force as visions, cloud chariots, and ghosts are revealed, as well as details of the construction of eighteenth-century sound effects equipment for the simulation of rain and thunder.

In a concluding chapter, the author discusses the playhouse designed for Richmond, Virginia, in 1798 by Benjamin Henry Latrobe. This imaginative building, years ahead of its time, was never constructed. The city of Richmond is now planning to build a slightly modified version of Latrobe's theater on a site not far from the one originally selected by the architect. Mr. McNamara illustrates Latrobe's plans and shows a model of the proposed theater as it will look when completed.